STEADFAST FAITH

A Guide For Christians In An Ailing Church

STEADFAST FAITH

A Guide For Christians In An Ailing Church

by

Todd H. Wetzel

Latimer Press
Solon, Ohio 44139

STEADFAST FAITH:
A Guide For Christians In An Ailing Church
© 1997 Latimer Press
All Rights Reserved

First Printing,
LATIMER PRESS
30325 Bainbridge Road
Building A, Suite 1
Solon, Ohio 44139
To Order: 1-800-553-3645

* All Scripture quotations, unless otherwise indicated, are taken
from the HOLY BIBLE, NEW INTERNATIONAL VERSION®. NIV®.
Copyright © 1973, 1978, 1984 by International Bible Society.
Used by permission of Zondervan Publishing House.
All rights reserved.

* All proceeds from this book including remuneration to the author are
designated to the work and ministry of Episcopalians United.

To my beloved wife and best friend Cherie and all of the many friends who have helped form my thoughts and encouraged my faith with deep appreciation

Acknowledgments

I wish to thank the many people who have provided support and assistance on this project.

Dr. and Mrs. Colvin Agnew
Mr. and Mrs. Olin Atkinson
Mr. and Mrs. Frederic E. Beck
Berkey Brendel Sheline
Mr. and Mrs. Nelson Black, Jr.
Dr. and Mrs. Hayes C. Byrne
Christ Episcopal Church (Plano, TX)
Mr. and Mrs. Thomas Cochran
Mr. and Mrs. Paul Correa
Mrs. Luciel L. Davidsen
Mr. and Mrs. Tom Davis
Mr. and Mrs. Calvin S. DeGolyer, Jr.
Mr. and Mrs. E. K. Delph
Mrs. Jack W. Drinnen
Mrs. Donald P. Duncan, Jr.
Rear Adm. and Mrs. Robert W. Durfey
Dr. and Mrs. David M. Fitzgerald
The Rev. Canon Loren Foot
Ms. Bonnie Forzly
Mr. Graydon C. Fox
Mr. and Mrs. Thomas Francis
Mr. and Mrs. William Lynch Fuller
Ms. Vivienne L. George
Mrs. John R. Gilliom
Dr. and Mrs. Duane I. Gillum
Mr. John S. Guthrie
Mr. David Hardy
Mr. Holman Head
Mr. and Mrs. Remsen B. Henry
Mr. and Mrs. James Houchin
Mrs. M. E. Jamieson
Ms. Francis Jenkins

Mr. and Mrs. John E. Jones
Mr. and Mrs. John M. Jones
Mr. and Mrs. Richard Lopez
Mrs. Leonard Lye
Mr. and Mrs. W. C. Marbaker
Mr. and Mrs. Albert Mehlman
Dr. Eston E. Melton, Jr.
Mr. Richard W. Michaels
Dr. Betty Young O'Dell
Dr. and Mrs. James Park
Mr. and Mrs. Joseph Pinto, Jr.
Mr. L. George Platt
Mr. and Mrs. Dudley Price
Mr. A. Crenshaw Reed, Jr.
Mr. and Mrs. Charles V. Robertson
Mr. Donald B. Root
Mr. and Mrs. Charles A. Schwartz
Mr. and Mrs. Jack Shaw
Mr. James Shouse
Mr. and Mrs. Rufus Smith
Mr. and Mrs. Gil Starkey
Mr. Seabury D. Stoneburner
Mr. and Mrs. Wally Taber
Dr. F. Mitchell Theisman
Mr. and Mrs. Frank H. Trane
The Rev. and Dr. B. W. Wait, III
Mr. and Mrs. Harold C. Wetzel
Mr. and Mrs. Randall C. Wetzel
Mrs. Todd H. Wetzel
The Rev. C. Bradley Wilson
Dr. and Mrs. Harold Wilson
Mrs. Lillie W. Wood

Table of Contents

Psalm 1

Blessed is the man
   who does not walk in the counsel of the wicked
or stand in the way of sinners
   or sit in the seat of mockers.
But his delight is in the law of the LORD,
   and on his law he meditates day and night.
He is like a tree planted by streams of water,
   which yields its fruit in season
and whose leaf does not wither.
   Whatever he does prospers.

Not so the wicked!
   They are like chaff
   that the wind blows away.
Therefore the wicked will not stand in the judgment,
   nor the sinners in the assembly of the righteous.

For the LORD watches over the way of the righteous,
   but the way of the wicked will perish.

1 Standing Firm On A Slippery Slope

*"Therefore, since we are surrounded by such a great
cloud of witnesses, let us throw off everything that
hinders and the sin that so easily entangles, and let us
run with perseverance the race marked out for us. Let
us fix our eyes on Jesus, the author and perfecter of
our faith ..."*

Hebrews 12:1, 2

It is no secret that for several years now, a small
cadre of men and women have been fighting a war
of propaganda by which they seek to radically alter
and revise the teaching and practice of Christianity in
the Episcopal Church.

And they're doing very well.

They have succeeded in winning over (or intimidating into silence) a substantial number of bishops, priests
and laity, to the point that our Church now seems headed in a direction far different from any we've mapped
out before — a road far wider than the narrow way
Jesus told us His followers they would have to walk
(Matthew 7:13-14).

Many within our denomination — looking down that

road and believing that its inevitable end is destruction
— ask me why they should walk along. They wonder
what, if anything, is left to bind a conservative conscience (with a sincere desire to be faithful) to the mud-
dled morality and apostate agenda of the Episcopal
Church.

There are other churches — good ones — churches
not nearly as besieged by the in-fighting and upheaval.
Why not leave the Episcopal Church to its obscured
vision and self-destructive choices?

That, of course, is a question every Church member
must pray through and decide for himself. Each of us
must follow God's direction as we sense it through the
Scriptures and through His Spirit in our hearts. We know
our Father's delight and desire is for unity in His Church
— and yet the Bible shows us that some are called out
to go and accomplish His purposes in new settings and
circumstances.

What I can confidently share with you in these
pages is the deepest conviction of my own heart — that
God is not through with the Episcopal Church. As bad
as things may appear right now, they have been much
worse in times past, and, even more importantly, there is
work that conservatives with a Christian conscience can
accomplish — in our personal relationships, in our local
parishes, among our bishops and Church leaders, and
even at the national level.

How can we do it? How can we begin to accomplish so tremendous and daunting a task? How do we
undertake to overhaul an entire denomination?

I trust we will see in the pages that follow that the
answer to this question is painfully, agonizingly simple.

We must overhaul ourselves. We must first analyze

the problems within the Church, for understanding must precede solutions. Once we can recognize and understand the challenges, then we can begin to formulate solutions and devise a path to follow.

Hebrews 12:1 lays out the prescription. There are great weights of guilt and grudge and prejudice and delusion that must be set aside.

There is sin from which we must disentangle ourselves — as individuals, and as a Church.

There is a race set before us that will require more endurance and grace and divine determination than anything we have experienced before.

And there is an example from which to draw wisdom and strength — Jesus Christ, Who with loving care has composed our days and our duty, and Who alone knows the finish of our faith.

In the pages to follow, I'd like to explore with you the weights that bear so heavily on the Church, the sins that have ensnared us, and the race I see laid out ahead. I'd like to join you in fine-tuning our focus on the Savior Who alone can lead us out of the moral wilderness His Church has wandered into.

But first, I'd like to give you a glimpse of my soul, a peek into the conscience of one of these "wild-eyed fanatic" conservatives — a sense of what has made me who I am and pierced me with a deep love for God and for the Episcopal Church.

It involves a remarkable cloud of witnesses.

"Therefore, since we are surrounded by such a great cloud of witnesses ..."

2 A Rich Inheritance

"I have been reminded of your sincere faith, which first lived in your grandmother Lois and in your mother Eunice and, I am persuaded, now lives in you also."

2 Timothy 1:5

Where did you come to your conviction of what it means to be a Christian? Who impressed upon you that this is pure and undefiled religion before God and the Father (James 1:27)?

I believe our love for Christ and for His Church is, at least in part, a reflection of our continuing love for those individuals who have come to epitomize it in our memory and experience.

Each of us carries within a composite profile of the ideal Christian, the collective portrait of the godly examples we have seen in those we watched, listened to, and came to respect. The ones who first excited us to believe that God is real and good and that the life to be found in Him was the only one worth living. The ones in whom faith was genuine, something more than a habit or a hobby or a high horse from which to look down on others.

I have been blessed to meet so many such believers, before and after my own conversion, but, like many other Christians, I treasure the memory of a handful who forged my enduring perception of what it means to believe, to live out that belief, and to model that belief through God's Church.

Some of my earliest and most cherished memories are of my great-grandfather Shaffer. A devout Christian layman, he rose at 5:30 every morning to step downstairs into the kitchen, light a fire in the stove, turn on a small light over the table, and read his Bible. Every morning, for as long as anyone in the family could remember, he was up with the dawn, sitting at that table, beseeching the Lord on behalf of his wife and his children, his grandchildren and his great-grandchildren — and his church.

Do you think those prayers made a difference? Do you think the quiet devotion of that lifetime left any lasting imprint on the souls of his family and the people of his parish?

I can tell you this. It made an enduring impact on me. I owe an incredible debt of gratitude to that good and godly man for a heritage of faith — and the faithful transmission of that faith from generation to generation. The deepest prayer of my heart is to leave my children and grandchildren a legacy like that.

As a child, I attended an Evangelical United Brethren Church. My grandmother and my great-aunt took me. "Remember, Todd," my grandmother would tell me, "wherever you go in life, Jesus goes with you." Those words have haunted me ever since. They have not, I'm deeply sorry to say, kept me from going into places and situations that Jesus would not have chosen to enter —

but they emblazoned on my soul a sense of a personal God and my personal responsibility to him for every choice I make.

A different but no less profound impression was carved into my childhood memory by Cora Mae Taylor, a retired missionary woman who had served for years in that mysterious, faraway land called China. As a little boy in the basement Sunday School of that Evangelical United Brethren Church, I had mixed feelings about Ms. Taylor. She was 88 years old, always wore black clothes and leaned hard on a cane, and at the time I thought she smelled funny, too.

She would come hobbling down the basement stairs, and they'd drag us out of our classrooms to hear her stories of China, and I'd sit listening to those strange words in that hard-to-understand voice, and wonder what in the world she was talking about.

She came down those stairs and talked to us pretty regularly over the next two years, an ancient servant of God facing a bored and reluctant audience. And gradually, my impressions of her changed. The smell and the hard-to-understand words faded in importance compared with the love and commitment and the joyful face of this dear woman, who kept rising up off her bed to limp down those stairs and tell us of the powerful, far-reaching love of Jesus.

That basement must have seemed, some Sundays, at least as far away as China itself for her, and no doubt the Chinese were more receptive to her teachings. But I will never forget the love — for her Lord and for telling His story — that brought her down to that room, time and again.

As long as some of those missionary stories could

be, I always looked forward to going to church when I was a boy. That's where Pastor Walker was. He greeted me every Sunday with a rich, warm smile. I could tell he was glad to see me, too. After services, if I was especially good, he would give me great pony-back rides down the center aisle of the church.

To this day, that man is my human image of what God is like. Through Pastor Walker's example, week in and week out, I came to think of church as a place where I could be happy, where I was loved, where I was special.

It was in large part through the combined influence of my grandmother, my great-aunt, and Pastor Walker that I accepted Jesus into my heart at the age of 12. The transparent joy of their faith drew me to taste of the waters of life for myself. And, as I grew older, the memory of that pastor in particular spurred me to the conviction that the pastorate could be a rich, rewarding and joyful calling.

In 1973, a year after I was ordained to the priesthood of the Episcopal Church, I went home to see my great aunt. While we were talking, she asked, "I have wondered why it is that you became a pastor?"

"Well, Aunt Helen," I said, "when I was a boy, Pastor Walker deeply touched my life. When I grew up I wanted to be just like him. He was a fine example of what being a clergyman is all about."

She looked at me with quizzical eyes.

"Pastor Walker? Oh, you mean Frank Walker. Todd, he was a layman."

That's how I discovered that my model of a pastor — my enduring example of pastoral ministry — wasn't even a pastor. Just a wonderful man who, in the life of one small child, had the kind of spiritual impact each of us would like to leave on the next generation.

The Episcopal Church today needs men and women who will make that kind of loving impact — whose integrity will be stamped on the children of this generation. Studies show that over 75 percent — 75 percent! — of the youngsters now growing up in the Episcopal Church will leave it as adults and never come back.

Some of them will find other church homes, perhaps. But many will forsake church involvement altogether. And the legacy that was lost to them:

- of devoted fathers and grandfathers, praying over their Bible;
- of loving families who delight in being a part of the Church;
- of retired missionaries whose faith still beams in their smiles;
- of kind laymen whose love for God and life embraces all they meet;

  ... will be lost to their children as well.

I don't want that to happen. I want our youth and children to learn love for God and for His Church the same way I did — through the lives of God's faithful, obedient people.

3 Hard Lessons

"As iron sharpens iron, so one man sharpens another."

Proverbs 27:17

Many seem convinced that a pastor's education ends with his completion of a seminary degree, if not before. In fact, some of the most searing and practical lessons I've learned in the Church have come through those I have met since entering the ordained ministry.

I was still a young clergyman when I received an invitation, along with 15 of my peers, to attend a conference led by Dr. Donald McGavran, an outstanding missionary and founder of the church growth movement. I attended that conference with a colleague from the Diocese of Ohio, a young man, I remember thinking, who had it all. He was handsome, sophisticated, intelligent, well-bred — a lifelong Episcopalian and a shining example of what a young clergyman should be.

Together, we worked through three days of discovery, analyzing the biblical principles of church growth and development. It was startling stuff — for many of us, it turned our whole world upside down. The unshakeable conclusion of our study was that the essence of church growth lay in active, fervent, church-wide evangelism — a dynamic, ongoing effort to introduce lost souls to Jesus Christ.

Not everyone was ready for that.

"Dr. McGavran," my friend said, standing to his feet. "Am I correct in understanding that what you are saying is that no church will grow unless people are personally committing themselves to Jesus Christ?"

"Young man," the former missionary replied, "you have it right."

"There has got to be another way," my friend said, "and I am going to find it."

He found something else instead. Today, he has left his church, left his wife, and spends most of his time "consulting." I believe he has abandoned a rich heritage of faith for a lie.

His tragic example confirmed for me the wisdom of the old missionary. There is only one path for those who love God and the Church, and that is through Jesus Christ. We cannot ignore His teachings, despise His example, disavow the realities of His birth, death and resurrection — and expect His transforming power to lift the Church out of its moral slump.

My friend tried to separate the character of the Church from the character of its Founder, and found that that's impossible.

The Rev. Albert (Abood) S. Sam taught me that lesson in a more inspiring way.

Father Sam and I went to seminary together. Quite a guy. He was a Syrian, with a heart as big as Texas and arms that stretched nearly as far, and those arms were always reaching out to hug somebody. His was a tender soul — he could be moved to tears in an instant. He wasn't much of a student, but he more than made up for it with his love and enthusiasm.

Those qualities served him and his Savior well in the pastorate. He loved his first congregation to life in Jesus Christ. He loved his second flock the same way.

Then came a serious heart attack. And, shortly afterward, the tragic death of his mother in a car accident. The difficulties kept coming and coming. Soon, Father Sam had to resign from parish ministry.

It was a lot for even his gentle soul to bear. And finally, one night at three in the morning, he had had enough.

He rolled out of his bed and stood before his God.

"Why have you let this happen to me?" he cried. "I am so angry with you I can't stand it!"

He was standing there, helpless in his pain and frustration and fury, when the idea flashed through his mind.

When his mother was angry, she made bread.

For the next six hours, Abood worked down in the kitchen, baking bread. He wound up with quite a few loaves, and no idea what to do with them.

He decided to give them away.

People liked the Syrian bread. They asked for more. They shared it with others, who asked for more. Father Sam kept baking.

Eventually, he founded a corporation: Father Sam's Syrian Bread. Today his bread is distributed in more than 20 states, and that number keeps growing. His corporation is worth multiplied millions of dollars.

A few years ago, Father Sam took all the stock in his company and divided it equally among his surviving children. Some outstanding business and legal advisers warned him: "You're crazy! There will be nothing to help work out disputes."

"I'll be there," he said.

"But you will no longer have any stock."

"If I cannot lead my family on the strength of my character and the ability to persuade them to the right cause," he said, "no amount of stock will change it."

Father Sam's example underscored for me the critical element of character — in my own daily life, and in the life of the Church I love. We cannot separate Christ's Church's character from that of the Savior Who founded it. Our moral choices as individuals and as a denomination must be grounded in the Scriptures. If we cannot build an effective Church on the strength of God's character and His revealed Word, we certainly won't be able to raise it by our own stubborn willpower.

The God Who turned Father Sam's anger and tears into bread — and that bread into a fabulously successful business — is the same God we serve. He is more than able to turn the hardened hearts of the Church's liberal leadership back to Himself — the Bread of Life — and to make the Church a success once more.

I know. I used to have a pretty hard heart myself.

After graduating from seminary, I worked in a parish in a prominent, well-to-do suburb on the west side of Cleveland. The parish was at the point of closing when my wife and I first went there, but great patience, hard work, and her gifts as a warm and enthusiastic hostess slowly turned the tide. Four years later, we had 550 members, and Church of the Advent was still growing.

The bishop thought we were doing a great job. My fellow clergymen congratulated me. The people of the parish loved us.

But some problems nagged at me. People weren't committing their lives to Christ. I saw no real signs of spiritual growth among our members. No one was being healed. And many couples were leaving the Church, afraid to expose their collapsing marriages and impending divorces to the congregation. It seemed there were no spiritual answers for them here.

Yet people continued to come past me at the door after services each Sunday, shaking my hand and smiling and saying, "Good sermon, Father."

Let me tell you, there's nothing worse than being told how good you are when you know how bad you are. And in my heart, I knew I wasn't doing a good job. I was failing God and His people.

But I, too, kept smiling and shaking hands, saying "Thank you. Thank you."

Until three events shattered my status quo.

4 The Great Awakening

"Better is open rebuke than hidden love."

Proverbs 27:5

My awakening came in three not so easy pieces. My first bolt from the blue came in the guise of two faithful women in the parish whom I knew had been praying diligently for me for four years.

They came to me one day and graciously, lovingly swung a wrecking ball into my illusions.

"Father Todd," they said, "we know you love the Lord, but we don't hear much about the Lord from the pulpit. We know that you study the Word of God, but there is not much of the Word in your teaching. We want to hear from the Lord — and we are going to keep praying for you."

Those words seared my heart. I found myself on my knees in my office, tears streaming down my face — for I knew to the depths of my soul that they were right.

"God," I prayed, "if this is what parish ministry is all about, I have to leave. I can't stand this any longer. You either have to change me or you have to change this parish.

"But God, I want you to know right now that I sur-render. I've had it. I can't go on like this any longer. My sense of failing you is eating me alive."

That was the beginning of a great turning-around — in my life, and in the life of that parish. The second fac-tor in my awakening to God's calling and purpose came with the umpteenth call from a charismatic Lutheran pastor.

He had been hounding me for four years to join him and several other charismatic pastors in the vicinity for a prayer breakfast. I had always refused, confident in my summa cum laude degree and the intelligence to which it testified. Speaking in tongues was for those who didn't know better.

His persistence finally dovetailed with my depression over the state of my ministry. I had promised him I'd be at the breakfast the next morning, come what may. And I showed up — to find only two men waiting. One was the Lutheran pastor.

The other was a Pentecostal pastor and retired mis-sionary who, like me, had never attended before. He looked at me and said, "You're Todd, aren't you?"

"Yes," I said. "Who are you?"

"I'm Pastor Ellerbee, and I have been praying for you for two-and-half years. When we've had breakfast, would you mind praying with me for awhile?"

After breakfast we went into the chapel to pray. I knelt down and that man began praying my life out over my head. He knew things about me that only God could have revealed. And the stone in my heart rolled away.

Nothing especially dramatic happened. I didn't fall down. I didn't roll around on the floor. I just stood up, filled with more joy and peace than I had experienced in a very long time. I slid into my car, drove down the road, and started to sing. It was the most natural thing in the world.

Then, suddenly, it hit me — this isn't English anymore. God had given me the gift of praising Him in other tongues.

And the more I sang, the happier I felt.

It showed. And showed. Over the next six months, God gave me a powerful gift of evangelism. Almost without fail, within 10 or 15 minutes of walking into a parish member's home, the whole family and I were on our knees praying for Jesus to come into their lives in a new and fresh way. For many of those members, it was their first real experience with the living Christ. A dramatic change began to roll through our suburban Episcopal parish. A sense of excitement and expectancy began to fill many hearts.

But not all. There were many who could not understand or appreciate the remarkable transformation — and one of them was my wife.

As far as she could tell, everything we had been doing together for the last four years was right. The changes in me and in our parish caught her off guard, and I seemed unable or unwilling to put what was happening in my heart into words she could fathom. Mutual frustration led to mutual anger.

People within the parish quickly picked up on the tension, and took sides. Those less enthusiastic about the surging changes rallied to my wife — and encouraged her to be their spokesperson. The wedge between us grew deeper. I went home from a day of conflicts within the parish to face the same battles all over again with my wife.

The battles got old. After six or eight months of tearing at each other, I had had enough. Things came to a roaring head one day just before I left for a prayer retreat. We yelled at one another awhile, then I said:

"I can't bear to live with this kind of conflict in the Church and in my home. It will not work. Unless you come to know Jesus the way I know Jesus, this marriage is over!"

And with that — feeling properly pious and miserable — I left for the prayer retreat.

I missed most of what the retreat director said, but I did hear him tell us to "Go off, find a place alone, and listen to the Lord." I found a clearing in the woods, white with new-fallen snow. I walked out into the center of it, knelt down, and began to cry.

"God," I asked, "why doesn't she love you like I love you?"

And — in an instant, clear as a bell — the words snapped back at me:

"Why don't you love her like I love her?"

I sat there a long moment or two, absolutely stunned. Then I got up, walked back and found the retreat leader, and told him I was leaving.

And I went home to learn to love my wife.

Along with all her flaws and weaknesses — which I had become oh-so-adept at uncovering and critiquing — I began to see again the beautiful woman who had first inspired my love. I saw again the best qualities of her character, the unique qualities that made her like no one else I'd ever known, her rich potential for touching others with the love of Jesus Christ.

I began loving her in Christ-like ways as best I could

imagine, forgiving her, serving her, encouraging her, sharing with her the yearnings of my soul.

One Sunday morning less than six months later, she came walking down the center aisle of the church. She knelt at the rail, looked me right in the eye, and said, "I want to come home to Jesus, too."

The healing of our marriage was the third element in my great awakening to what it really means to be a Christian, a pastor, a leader in the Church I have loved so dearly for so long. Increasingly, in recent days, I come back to that long-ago experience with my wife as I look at the problems facing Christ's Church today, at my personal responsibility in dealing with those problems, and at the rich potential for ministry that I believe is still available to us as Episcopalians.

5 Irreconcilable Differences?

"Blessed are you when people insult you, persecute you and falsely say all kinds of evil against you because of me. Rejoice and be glad."

Matthew 5:11-12a

Sometime I don't feel especially blessed to be a priest and member of this Episcopal Church of ours.

Within the span of my years in the priesthood (1972-present), our Church has moved into a rancorous debate between liberalism and conservatism that threatens to divide the Church.

Liberalism has helped inform and guide our Church for over a hundred years. It has led us to a deeper commitment to and a greater compassion for society and the needs of our fellow human beings. That kind of "liberality of spirit" is a glory to God — and a corrective we will always need. The Church will always need those who prod it out of lethargy and hypocrisy and stir the fires of compassion. To freely offer your love of God and your gifts in service to humanity, that is one thing. But, to seek to diminish the Word of God written in the process, is quite another.

The definition of the term "liberal" has changed. Classic liberals have just about become extinct over these past three or four decades in the Episcopal Church. Once seen as "compassionate seekers of Truth," today's self-styled "liberals" have abandoned the Bible as the Word of God written and embraced both relativism and an often cynical view of religion. The real driving force of modern day liberalism in the Church is a passionate desire to redefine and revise Christianity. Liberalism has lost hold of the guiding parameters of historic Anglican thought, which — until recently — were roomy enough to hold both conservatives and classic liberals together, namely, Scripture, tradition, and reason, as guided by the Holy Spirit.

Conservatives still maintain the classic guiding parameters of Anglicanism. The 39 Articles, the Creeds, the Lambeth Quadrilateral (see *The Book of Common Prayer*, pgs. 864-878). For conservatives, the Bible does not simply contain God's words, nor is it the story of man's journey in spirituality. The Bible is the revealed Word of God "containing all things necessary to salvation" and is the rule and ultimate standard of faith. Today's liberals and conservatives have left the arena of differences of opinion and polite debate and entered into a struggle that involves both the soul and the future of our Church. And, that struggle has grown rancorous.

Some dangerous illusions are clouding the ongoing debates between liberals and conservatives over the future of the Church.

One is that all liberals — and all conservatives — are alike. This is sheer bigotry. Through the years, as I've traveled, I have been privileged to discover the Lord Jesus Christ living and working in the lives of a host of men, women and young people who love Him, though not always in the same way I do. Not all of them have been conservatives — or even evangelicals or charismatics. Some of them have even been liberals. Yet all of them have helped me delight in the Lord and grow in my relationship with Him.

If one is liberal with their love for God, their gifts and their service to humanity, that's one thing. If one is liberal with God's truth and commandments, that is quite another.

By the same measure, a person who is conservative with God's truth — but even more so with their love and generosity — is as far a cry from God's ideal as any apostate.

No, both the liberals and the conservatives within our Church must get past their illusions about each other. More than that, we must get over our illusions about ourselves.

Conservatives, for instance, must give up the notion that if we gain control of the governing apparatus of the Church, all will be well. Let's not be naive: even if we swept the administrative and executive offices tomorrow, the influence of liberalism would continue to be powerfully felt. Given the footing liberals now have throughout the Church, we would probably continue to suffer legislative losses. But even if we were running the Church, I suspect we might do just as bad a job as the current leadership is doing, if left to our own devices.

That's why conservatism must not primarily be about winning.

It's about preserving and defending and putting forward the truth.

Liberals, too, have forgotten about the truth. They

have convinced themselves that basic theology is not nearly so important as unity (even a false unity — a kind of ecclesiastical cease-fire agreement). It's most important, liberals say, that Christians embrace everybody, no matter what their beliefs — as long as those beliefs aren't conservative.

In other words, liberals have become dogmatic about opposing all dogma.

Many have also become arrogant, so that liberalism, as the Reverend Dr. Alistair McGrath — speaking at the Anglican Institute in the Spring of 1996 — has observed, now "appeals to a rapidly-decreasing circle of the culturally elite. Its proponents, such as Bishop Spong, are simply out of touch and naive. There is a fundamental disconnect between much of the [liberal] leadership in our Church and the people in the pews. Further, it is increasingly obvious that the best insights of liberal theology do not suffice to nourish a minority Church in an increasingly secular society."

Which brings us to a third illusion liberals and conservatives are prey to — the illusion that their particular perceptions of the Church are the only accurate reflections of reality.

Dietrich Bonhoeffer said, "When the morning mists of dreams have vanished, then dawns the basis of true Christian community."

Translation: "Beware of loving your dream of the Church more than the Church itself."

I believe that many liberals and conservatives are in love with their dreams. They are living their dream for the Church rather than living God's calling for the Church. We have — liberal and conservative alike — forgotten the very nature of the Church we serve. We have forgotten the character Christ has prescribed for that Church.

I listen to the conservatives who say about their liberal counterparts, "Oh God, why don't they love you like we love you?" I believe many liberals, looking at conservatives, breathe the same prayer. In secular terms, this would be grounds for divorce. However irreconcilable the differences between these two parties of the Church, divorce is not the solution. We have an obligation to remain together — for the sake of our common heritage, our long tradition of tolerance and for the sake of the living Lord Jesus Christ. I believe that God, listening to this prayer is whispering back to us, "Why don't you love the people of the Church — including them — like I love them?"

What a horrible thing it would be for history to record that Episcopalians "loved the Lord, but could not love one another."

In our concern for doctrines, many conservatives are learning to hate those on the other side of the breach. In their push for unity, many liberals are learning to hate those who take biblical doctrine and church traditions seriously. Neither side can justify that enmity in the name of Christ. The world must see our love for each other as a reflection of God's love for us. Both "liberals" and "conservatives" in our Church must reach across the gulf between us, trusting that truth will triumph.

This kind of coming together will be difficult to accomplish. The Lord has placed before us a challenge bigger than any one of us, or collection of us, for a purpose. He wants to drive us to our knees. He wants us to seek Him and learn to rely on His guidance.

In following Him daily, we will learn to love one

another.

Does that mean conservatives should set aside our convictions, sit back and smile on whatever the liberals say, ignoring the teachings of the Bible and the dictates of our own conscience?

Of course not.

We cannot stop contending for and affirming the truth of the Gospel and biblical morality — even when that truth is unpopular. For, one of the deepest convictions of Christianity is that Truth and Christ are one and the same. As we all draw nearer to Christ, we will all draw nearer to the Truth. Christ will ultimately prevail — indeed, is even now prevailing! Truth, too will prevail, whether at the next General Convention or the one my grandchildren attend.

But, we must not forget the story of the Apostle John, the beloved disciple, who in the closing years of his life was so enfeebled by age that he could hardly speak. The Christian community carried him from congregation to congregation. To each, the aged apostle breathed the same simple three-word sentence, "Love one another." This is our marching order and the longer we disobey, the more damage is done.

This damage could affect eternity, through the souls the Church misleads, or ignores.

McGrath says theological liberalism will either die or lead the Church into death. That sounds harsh. But, let's examine the present condition of the Episcopal Church.

6 The Trouble With Episcopalians

"I know your deeds, that you are neither cold nor hot. I wish you were either one or the other!"

Revelation 3:15

Looking at the Church today, I am reminded of James Madison, the first bishop of the Diocese of Virginia (1790-1812) and President of the College of William and Mary. The state of the Episcopal Church fell rapidly in the years following the American Revolution. While an active churchman, Madison despaired over the condition of his diocese, making only one visitation in the diocese. Only 15 clergy and laymen attended the Virginia Diocesan Convention in 1805.

Seven years passed before the next diocesan convention, and Virginia failed to send any representatives to four successive General Conventions. The General Convention of 1808 spoke of the Virginia Diocese, "there is danger of her total ruin." Then Chief Justice Marshall observed that the church was "too far gone to be revived."

Some days, a lot of us within the Episcopal Church feel the same way. Looking around at what has so quickly become of our once strong and vibrant denomination, we have to wonder what happened — and if there's really any hope for the future.

Bishop Madison must have asked those same questions especially during the years of his episcopacy.

But there's a "rest of the story."

On May 5, 1814, some two years after the death of Bishop Madison, Richard Channing Moore was elected second Bishop of Virginia and soon brought new life into the diocese through his evangelical preaching and great zeal. Soon the Diocese of Virginia was thriving once more, and the rest of the Episcopal Church was "on the grow" with her.

My friend, it can happen again.

I do believe there is hope — and I am eager to share that hope with you. But we can't build the Church we're dreaming of until we confront the realities of the Church as it is. And so, a short overview of eight problems I believe are at the root of so much of our current frustration and failure — problems we as a Church are going to have to confront and deal with if we are ever to have any impact on a lost and dying world.

1) The majority of our Episcopal laity do not understand and cannot intelligently discuss the most important issues of Christianity: salvation through Jesus, morality, Church polity, liturgical change and theology.

Most of our members are in the dark about issues beyond the boundaries of their own parishes. And, frankly, most prefer it that way. Local clergy, in their desire to minimize potential conflict, often contribute to laity remaining in the dark by failing to share or discuss or preach on controversies occurring in the wider

Church.

2) Much of our clergy — though well-equipped to function as chaplains — are poorly equipped to be evangelists, teachers and preachers.

For centuries, ministers ministered and congregations congregated, and that was enough. But circumstances have radically changed within the last 50 years. We are no longer a Christian culture. We cannot minister effectively as a Church if we are training workers and preparing laymen for a Christendom that no longer exists. We have to admit that the playing field has radically altered — and that, by and large, we have failed to change with it.

3) Many members of our deeply dedicated clergy are men and women who want to serve but who also seek to avoid conflict at any cost.

Seminary inculcates many of our clergy with a sense of loyalty to the institutional Church, and too often they view their loyalty to the Church as identical with their loyalty to Christ because the Church is defined as the body of Christ. But no Church is righteous, only Christ is righteous.

Yet service in a hierarchical system — whether it be the Episcopal Church, the Anglican Church of Canada or the United Church of Canada — has produced a lifestyle of accommodation, compromise and envy in far too many clergy. They have sacrificed a willingness to take risks for the security of a career — a career that depends on their willingness to curry favor with both their congregation and denominational executives.

The inevitable result: many of our clergy have become far too timid and accommodating.

4) Many of our bishops have failed to exhibit

spiritual and moral oversight.

Add this to the growing timidity of the clergy, and you see a clear recipe for disaster.

The office of bishop has become secularized — and its attainment grossly politicized. Many executives (in our case, bishops) are good leaders, good people whose gifts are buried under the demands of administration. Some can and do lead, but most seem too isolated and ill-equipped to do so effectively. They have forgotten an important maxim from our Lord: "And whoever wants to be first must be slave of all" (Mark 10:44).

In the Episcopal Church, we have inherited a centuries-old style of princely leadership. We need to correct that old model with a new one: servant leadership. Too many of our bishops function like petty princes of the Church rather than servants in the household of God.

Accountability is a difficult concept for some of these men and women to grasp, although many demand it from their clergy. In desperation, a number of bishops now look to the House of Bishops for mutual support and understanding. In their ardent (and understandable) desire for fellowship, many have been willing to sacrifice obedience to their primary vow — the vow to defend the Faith. For too many in the House of Bishops, unity has become a far more important goal than the pursuit of truth and the discipline of the Gospel.

(In truth, I suspect this problem is not limited to our bishops. I suspect it is something that denominations and denominational bureaucracies have fallen into all too readily throughout the Christian church today.)

5) The nature of the Church is changing.

For all of us in the West — whether it be Canada, the United States, England, Germany — centralized bureaucratic structures are breaking down, in favor of more local, horizontal styles of management. Resources of money and talent no longer flow up the hierarchy as they once did. Instead, we are becoming what we once were — loose federations of local congregations whose great strength lies not in denominational structures but *in the congregations themselves*. In reality, congregational life is the wellspring of all our Church's resources. Much of what is good in the Church flows from that spring.

6) We are not challenging — or fully utilizing — our lay people.

Many churches are still placing laity in old church roles, which do nothing to increase their faith or encourage them to share it, let alone train them and equip them to do so. Our Church has not sufficiently addressed the subject of lay ministry, but to be effective, it must do so. It must raise up clergy who will fire the imagination and inspire the participation of their parish members. We desperately need a new kind of clergy leadership that knows how to bless lay leadership.

7) We have not yet learned how to incorporate the Bible into the decision-making processes and discussions of our churches.

Those on the religious right in the U.S. pride themselves on taking the Bible literally, while those on the left take Scripture primarily as myth and metaphor. I believe both sides fail to take the Bible seriously.

More than that, most of our people don't read it. We have, as yet, failed to find ways to encourage and guide lay people in the discovery of the premier Book of books. The Bible leads only as God's people seek guidance from God within its words. We need to learn how to take the Bible seriously in all of our gatherings, and most especially, when we come together to make decisions.

8) There is a mistaken concept among Episcopalians that peace and harmony are the norm rather than conflict.

Where two or three are gathered together, the Scriptures promise, Christ Jesus will be in the midst of them — and so will conflict. He sets the dividing line between the world and the kingdom of God. Therefore wherever He goes, there will be conviction, conversion and conflict.

We treat the current state of conflict within the Church as a gross aberration of the norm, but a brief reading of the Book of Acts, and even a cursory glance at the history of the Church, bears witness to the truth that we are a body of people for whom conflict is the norm. We live in a secular culture with shifting relative values, a short attention span and a highly self-centered concept of the person. Of course a Christian is going to provoke conflict!

Conflict is inevitable and necessary if one is to mature as a Christian. Christ loved everyone, but it is clear from the record that not everyone loved Christ. What was true for the Master, He said, will be true for the disciple — and so it has been. Not only in the year 50 A.D., not only in the Dark Ages, but now — today — in an age that is itself getting darker all the time.

7 In The Dark

"But if your eyes are bad, your whole body will be full of darkness. If then the light within you is darkness, how great is that darkness!"

Matthew 6:23

Sometimes, it's hard to tell a sunrise from a sunset.

Especially if you don't know which direction you're looking.

That's the situation today for our Church. Episcopalians right now are moving in a strange twilight of changing morality and shifting foundations. Many of our laypeople seem confused about what direction we're heading in, and many of our clergy and leaders haven't made up their mind, either.

Time will soon reveal the truth, though — whether we are about to find more light, or plunge deeper into the darkness.

I, for one, believe it's getting darker. As a nation and as a Church, I believe, we are making choices that will darken the path before us and obscure our ability to make the maximum impact on a lost world.

But, though I sometimes feel a great deal of frustration and anger — I am not in despair. I am not predicting defeat.

Somebody once said to me, "You know, it's getting darker in here."

"Good!" I said. "That makes it easier to see the light."

And, that's where we are today. It is getting darker so that the light of Christ may be more easily seen — so people can find the light again.

But make no mistake — it's getting darker. The darkness that has fallen across our American culture has seeped into the Church.

In the last 100 years, a radical transformation has taken place in our society. The United States has become a mission field in itself. We live in a nation that knows less and less about belonging to a church, one that is ignorant of the Gospel and unaware of its biblical heritage.

A nation that no longer recognizes faith as the glue that holds life together in a meaningful way.

A nation that no longer understands the necessity for salvation.

A nation that no longer acknowledges its need for God.

Our nation has rebelled against God, and forgotten Him. Now I believe He is letting it get darker and darker so that we might see and recognize the light once more.

That growing darkness is revealed in three specific trends:

1) Roughly half of the population of the U.S. is now unchurched.

Fifty years ago, everybody had at least a vague notion of what church was about. Most people were nominally

Christian and part of a Christian culture. Today that is no longer true.

Of course, if half of our population does *not* participate in a local church, that means the other half *does*. Even among the half of our population which does not (about 125 million people), one-third of them are still able to identify a church if pressed for the information: "Yeah, I go to Parker Road Methodist Church." But this is really a statement of the church they *don't* go to, the one where they show up once or twice a year, Christmas and Easter, and possibly for an occasional baptism, wedding or funeral.

Another one-third of our unchurched population can't identify a specific church, but they can name their denominational affiliation or at least declare whether they are Protestant or Roman Catholic. But ask them what it means to be a Protestant or Catholic, and they have no idea. They only know that some time ago their parents attended a Protestant church, or their grandparents were Roman Catholic.

The final one-third of our unchurched, roughly 41 million, have no sense of what church is about at all. They don't really know what people are talking about when they mention "the church." They represent a wide-open field for evangelism.

What do these statements mean in terms of church life? Through the 1950's, churches grew pretty much on their own, and very little evangelism needed to take place. Families were at least nominally Christian, and we didn't have to spend much time explaining what it meant to be Christians except in Sunday School and confirmation classes.

Today, society is ignorant of what we're talking about

when we mention the mission of Jesus. When we declare that Jesus died on a cross for sins or died in order to give life abundantly, the culture stares blankly and says, "Huh?" That means today's churches have really become missionary bases, sending members out to their communities to do basic evangelism. Both clergy and laity alike must begin to see themselves as missionaries in a culture alien to Christianity. In today's culture, the church which is not involved in that mission is a dying church.

Most Episcopalians are in what could be loosely categorized as progressive-liberal churches, and they believe that their congregations are typical/normative. The facts confirm that the very things many members in our churches have been taught to debunk and devalue, are the very things which plant and grow healthy churches both at home and in other parts of the world.

In the broader context of 20th century international Christianity, there is a wonderful story of faith to be told. The Anglican Church and the Christian Church are each growing at an unprecedented rate. Africa is founding churches every week, and new dioceses every month. In Asia the Church is growing on a massive basis. (Along with this growth comes persecution. There have been more martyrs for Christ in the 20th century than in all previous centuries put together.) Fundamentalism — defined as an affirmation of the fundamentals of faith — is growing. *And* where the fundamentals are affirmed, the Church grows.

2) The growth of mega-churches.

Of the 350,000 churches in the United States, half of them have fewer than 75 people in attendance on Sunday. But 51 percent of all people in attendance on

Sunday morning go to 14 percent of the churches. In other words, most Americans who attend a church regularly now do so in churches whose average Sunday attendance exceeds 400 people.

This is a trend toward "mega-churches" which did not exist in the past. Let me give you a comparable statistic. In the early 1930's, there were more than 130,000 school boards in America. Today, there are fewer than 15,000, and the population is considerably larger. The history of education in America has been the consolidation of bigger and bigger school districts with larger schools, on the theory that schools could be run more efficiently and effectively. Whether these "mega-schools" and "mega-districts" have proved their worth over one-room schoolhouses of the past (or even today's smaller, private institutions) is debatable.

Have the mega-churches proven their worth? In fact, it doesn't matter because the probable trend of churches in the U.S. over the next 25 years will include a continuum of the closing of more and more small churches in favor of fewer, larger ones. Church as we understand it — and as increasingly younger generations understand it — cannot be maintained with a congregation of 75 people. Small churches cannot hire the staff or field the volunteers to do the kind of programs that baby-boomers require (and which, in all likelihood, their children and grandchildren will require). It's difficult to have a good Sunday School when you have only 75 people from which to staff it. It's difficult to have a good marriage support system when there are only 75 people to draw from. It's difficult to put together Christian life ministries and programs when there is such a small group of people to staff them. Our churches simply require more people to do the kinds of ministries that most of us feel we need for our own spiritual growth. As a result, we will hear of more church closings and see more big churches. The years ahead will be a period of consolidation.

The Episcopal Church does not have many mega-churches, but many small, personal, local congregations. Sadly, our denomination is in grave danger of a drastic decline during this consolidation period if we do not start growing through evangelism and discipleship.

3) People increasingly distrust institutions.

In society at large, we are skeptical of our institutions — political, educational, religious — and the motives of our leaders. We no longer automatically believe that they can or will serve our interests.

As a result, more and more people are dropping out of big institutions. We use them sparingly and join fewer of them. In fact, for many, the primary goal (and only reason for) joining an institution is networking — building a web of relationships that support and sustain us, further our careers, open up opportunities for us and our families.

This results in carelessness regarding which church to join and minimizes denominational loyalty, since learning and following the teachings of the denomination are not the primary goals of joining the church institution. Networking takes precedence over piety. Questions about church membership — Were you baptized as an infant in the Episcopal Church? Was your last church membership in an Episcopal Church? Will your next church be an Episcopal Church? — are no longer considerations for many.

Growing churches find that more and more members

are looking for a church where Jesus is central to the life and ministry of that particular congregation. Denominational loyalty is not perceived as essential for proclaiming the Gospel of Jesus Christ.

Another symptom of the mistrust of institutions is the growing taxpayer revolt in this country. We want our money to be connected to our decisions. Current surveys show that older generations — people born before 1945 — give to *institutions*. Those born later give to *visions, needs* and *causes*. They want to see results and have a hand in them.

In light of these three assertions regarding the entire population of our nation — that many are unchurched, that most who attend church attend "mega-churches," and that the population as a whole mistrusts institutions — let's look specifically at the Episcopal Church.

8 The Darkness Grows

"You are the salt of the earth. But if the salt loses its saltiness, how can it be made salty again? It is no longer good for anything, except to be thrown out and trampled by men."

Matthew 5:13

What are the trends toward darkness in our own Church?

Trend No. 1: Our leadership has grown out of touch with the people in the pews.

Both a 1990 Gallup Survey and Episcopalians United's own 1989 survey of 100,000 households reveal that the ethics and morality of the person in the pew are not represented by the leadership.

For instance, the average person in the pews believes Jesus Christ is "the way, the truth and the life." (We are a more Christian denomination than most people ever suspected.) Unfortunately, roughly 50 percent of our clergy believe that Jesus is *a* way, not *the* way. Unlike their parishioners, they do not believe Christ was speaking definitively when he declared, "No one comes to the Father except through me" (John 14:6).

Yet this faithless leadership has an inordinate amount of power in matters of Episcopal Church governance. Ninety-nine percent of the people who attend Episcopal Churches are laypeople; one percent is clergy. However, in the national church, only 25 percent of the vote is cast by laity. Clergy cast the other 75 percent!

At the national level, all legislation is decided in two houses: a House of Deputies and a House of Bishops. The House of Bishops is made up entirely of clergy, as is half of the House of Deputies. Only one-half of one legislative house is made up of laity. The two houses must agree in order for any legislation to be carried out. Obviously, the clergy dominate the decision-making process.

And when you consider that the majority of the clergy are out of touch with the beliefs and desires of the laity, you clearly see how many of the decisions can go directly against what the vast majority of Episcopalians want and believe to be right.

There are many thousands of laypeople who believe in the future of this Church and who want to share in the ministry of Jesus Christ *through* the Episcopal Church. Laypeople have much to say, and they should not tolerate being denied the right to speak and be heard. The mind of Christ is not reserved solely for the ministers in black shirts.

As Executive Director of Episcopalians United, I am in contact every day with faithful Episcopalians who feel their beliefs are being trampled by clergy who don't even seem to belong in the same denomination or cherish the same tenets of faith. I am often told by the liberal-revisionist leadership that the only people who make this complaint (and join conservative organizations like

Episcopalians United) are people on the "fringes" of this Church, the older, the poorly-educated, the poorly-read, the parish dissidents.

Bishop John Shelby Spong was asked why churches with a conservative/traditional message of the Gospel were growing while liberal churches were shrinking drastically. "What that means to me," he said, "is that people who are thinking are leaving the church, and people who aren't thinking are going back." With that, he confirmed the prejudice of some bishops that only the poor or ignorant could believe the Gospel and affirm the traditions of the Church.

The facts tell a different story. Our surveys demonstrate that the people who join Episcopalians United are people of every age, educational background, and socio-economic status who have serious concerns about the direction in which our leadership is taking the Church. They are, in fact, the mainstream of the Episcopal Church in America:

- Our membership is split about evenly between men and women (the national Church is 57 percent female and 43 percent male).
- Over two-thirds of the contributing membership of our ministry have graduated from college (compared to only 52 percent in the Church at large).
- The median income of our members is considerably higher than the national Church's median of $30,000.
- Seventy-eight percent of our membership is married.
- Ninety-two percent of our members attend their local church regularly. They are con-

cerned and involved with the Episcopal Church — while the national average for attendance and participation among Episcopalians is only 40 percent.

Our membership is composed of Episcopalians who are mature, financially secure, well-educated, married and, by and large, white collar. They attend church much more frequently than the average Episcopalian, attend Bible study better than twice as often. Far from being on the fringes, they are the very heart of the Church. Yet these are the people who have been forced — by the decidedly non-scriptural direction the denomination has taken — to band together on behalf of preserving the traditional Church.

They *are* the Church, yet their beliefs are being ignored by a clergy which fails to represent them at the national level. One discouraged Episcopalian wrote to me:

> I simply cannot bring myself any longer to encourage anyone to become a member of the Episcopal Church and have concluded finally that I must leave it in order to do the work Christ would have me do. My own spirit has been wearied almost to exhaustion by the gross departure from Christ's teachings which we have seen in the Episcopal Church in recent years, with worse to come. It is simply no longer part of the "company of faithful people." I feel more and more that I am dealing with people who are spiritually insane.

Those of us who occupy the pews, who pray and pay the bills, differ radically in belief from our leadership. That's grounds for a revolution. But the revolution may not come. People are wary of institutions — and rather than try to reform a Church which does not represent them, they may drop out or become silent at the denominational level.

Trend No. 2: Our Church is fragmenting.

For many reasons — including the fact that our church leadership no longer represents our church membership — the Episcopal Church, nationwide, seems to have no consistent message. When you attend an Episcopal Church for the first time, you don't know whether you will hear the Gospel of Christ powerfully preached and demonstrated, or whether the priest will communicate that we live in a post-Christian world, that Jesus is just one of many religious teachers and that the Church is open to a diverse set of viewpoints and beliefs.

This message won't work in evangelizing today's world. The people of modern America have learned open-mindedness and tolerance for all beliefs as well as they have learned the alphabet and arithmetic in school. There's nothing life-changing in that message that they should want for themselves.

And proclaiming such a post-Christian pantheistic message damages the ministry of Episcopal Churches which preach only the Gospel — because both are labeled "Episcopal," and it appears that we as a denomination do not have a consistent message or bedrock faith at all. The denominations which are growing today are those that have a clear handle on the Gospel and are consistently reaching people for Christ.

Even Bishop Spong seems to see that the division between the liberal and conservative movements has pulled the Church apart — although he seems unconcerned by the implications of that fragmentation and disparages conservative, growing churches:

> The churches that are growing don't understand the issues, so they can traffic in old-fashioned certainty. They can convince people that they, and they alone, are right, and that is terribly appealing. The churches that are declining do understand the issues. They are embracing the relativity of truth; they feel like they have no message, and they don't have any message. So they are declining. (*United Voice*, January 1994, pg. 7).

The spiritual significance of that statement — of a church with no enduring message — seems lost on Bishop Spong.

But he is not alone. Many Episcopalians do not seem to have a clear grasp on the true purpose of the Church and how it must be structured in these modern days. In surveys that Gallup and others have conducted, about 89 percent of the respondents declared that the purpose of the Church is to meet their needs and serve their families. Some 11 percent responded that the purpose of the Church is to win the world for Christ.

When a huge majority selfishly believe the Church is here to serve me (rather than the other way around), how can we expect to see growth? The growing churches in this country are those that see themselves as mission stations charged with winning the world for Christ. They stand as outposts in a world that desperately needs Jesus.

Recently another shattering blow compounded the trend toward total fragmentation of our Church. The Court for the Trial of a Bishop dismissed both counts against Bishop Walter Righter in May, 1996 — counts that charged he ordained Barry Stopfel, a noncelibate homosexual man. Righter was called on to answer for action clearly against Church doctrine. The Court ruled that Title IV of the Episcopal Church's "Constitution and Canons" protects only a minimal "core doctrine" of the Church — in effect, demoting marriage from a sacrament to what the Court calls a "doctrinal teaching." Optional, apparently. This decision condemns the Church to further anarchy and conflict.

Both Holy Scripture and *The Book of Common Prayer* clearly teach the doctrine that Christians are to reserve sexual intimacy for the sacrament of marriage, yet the highest leadership of our Church cannot accept that. Instead they have affirmed the practice of homosexuality in flagrant violation of a Christian belief held by most of the membership.

The Church cannot abandon its essential doctrines without wreaking havoc in the lives of its members.

In an article for *The Vail Daily* entitled "Does Diversity in Christian Belief Include Ordaining Gays?"(June 8, 1996), Presbyterian commentator the Rev. Dr. Jack R. Van Ens has described such shifting sands of doctrine in terms of an analogy taken from the Mississippi River.

> For the river to remain a major maritime commercial waterway, both the shoals and the shipping lanes must be defined. Without the Mississippi River's shores marked, ships could be grounded on the shoals.

> Although the river is broad, the commerce on it easily gets congested. When lanes are not honored, ships crash into each other. Episcopal tradi-

tion leaves the river of belief open as wide as possible. Only the shores, over which the wreckage of wrong belief rots, are marked.

I would suggest that now we are not even marking the shores, for our most basic issues of right and wrong are being undermined in some arenas. In the Righter case, for instance, the Court compared our doctrine of marriage to past opinions about slavery!

This is ridiculous. Although all too many bishops sought to justify slavery, the Church never had a *doctrine* of slavery. You could search *The Book of Common Prayer* in vain for a slavery rite, or an Article of Religion which identifies slavery as a sacrament.

Yet the Court has denied the sanctity of marriage, in spite of its scriptural and doctrinal roots as a sacrament of our faith. With one decision, they have made a mockery of all the honest Episcopalians who have made vows of love and stood by them down through the years. Given such a radical ruling, how can the Church call for fidelity in any instance? On what basis will it ask priests to honor the sanctity of marriage? With this ruling, the Episcopal Church as a national entity plunges even more rapidly down its path of dissolution.

The Church's trend toward accommodating itself to the culture — rather than challenging the culture to conform to Scripture — is speeding up the fragmentation. The evidence abounds:

- General Theological Seminary declared that homosexual students no longer have to live by the traditional Christian teaching that sexual intercourse is appropriate only within marriage (whether they will extend this ruling to heterosexual students remains to be seen).

- Declining to affirm Jesus Christ as "the way, the truth and the life" or the unique Son of God, diocesan conventions have chosen the watered-down theology of Unitarianism over the revealed truth of Scripture.
- Episcopalians gathered at the Cathedral of Saint John the Divine, New York City, on Saint Francis Day and invoked the names of pagan gods in their prayers.
- The Episcopal Church in Minnesota has elevated James Jelinek to the position of Bishop of Minnesota — Jelinek had previously promised to begin ordaining practicing homosexuals to the clergy.

Ironically, this determination to open the front doors of belief wider and wider so that more and more people may join in has the effect of opening the back doors wider, too. More and more people are fleeing from this flimsy faith to find a church where the truth of the Gospel is actually taught and honored.

People understand that a church that stands for everything ultimately stands for nothing. This is the hard truth of recent decades: people leave the Episcopal Church in droves when the Church stops challenging them to live by the demanding morality of the Scripture. When the Episcopal Church merely reflects the surrounding culture, rather than confronting the surrounding culture's sin and calling for repentance, many men and women wonder why they should remain Episcopalians.

If you have been feeling confused by the disparity between what the media reports about the Episcopal Church and what you are hearing in your own parish church — you have a right to be. The Church is fragmenting as we speak. One reason for that breakup is the clergy's ignorance of (and disregard for) the membership's beliefs. Another reason is perhaps the most definitive issue — and certainly the darkest of the trends — we'll discuss here:

Trend No. 3: Scriptural authority is being challenged by the liberal/revisionist-leaning leadership of the Church.

The Rev. David Scott of Virginia Theological Seminary says, "God has established certain norms and standards for our pilgrimage: Scripture, tradition and reason. One of the fundamental facts of the life of the Church in our time is a profound confusion about those terms."

He goes on:

What I see happening is a fundamental shift —
from seeing these standards as external guides to
seeing them as inside of us. By this new view of
reason, and the added standard of experience,
some Episcopalians proceed to judge Scripture
and tradition.

In recent years, much of the Episcopal Church leadership has called for doctrine which makes personal experience an authority equal to that of the Scriptures. For instance, when General Theological Seminary freed homosexual students from biblical standards of sexual purity, they did so citing Resolution 104-A from 1991's General Convention, which acknowledges "discontinuity between this teaching and the experience of many members of this body."

In other words, if you have sinned and enjoyed it, then your enjoyment carries weight equal to (or weightier than) the Scripture which forbids sin. Our leadership seems to forget that if our experience is as authoritative as the Bible, we have no means of distinguishing between the Holy Spirit and the spirit of our age.

Those who look to scriptural authority regarding decision-making in the Church are now called "conservatives." As such, we believe the Bible is the inspired Word of God. Our historic Anglican approach to Scripture is indicated in the Articles of Religion. Article 8 states that we believe the Creeds only because "they may be proved by most certain warrants of Scripture." Article 20 says that "It is not lawful for the Church to ordain anything that is contrary to God's Word written." Article 34 says that the Church traditions and customs must be subject to the authority of Scripture. The affirmation of the primary authority of Scripture is central to any description of the Episcopal faith.

And this is what the majority of Episcopalians believe.

We believe that the moral standards for Christians are clearly laid out in Scripture. Further, we believe that God, through the Scriptures, has defined Himself in ways which are unchangeable.

As Episcopalians, we regularly join in praying, "Blessed Lord, who caused all holy Scriptures to be written for our learning: Grant us so to hear them, read them, mark, learn, and inwardly digest them, that we may embrace and ever hold fast the blessed hope which you have given us in our Savior Jesus Christ; who lives and reigns with you and the Holy Spirit, one God, for ever and ever" (*The Book of Common Prayer*, p.236, Proper 28).

Yet the Episcopal leadership seems intent on discounting Scripture whenever it suits them — on issues ranging from inclusive language in the psalms and liturgy to the ordination of practicing homosexuals.

9 A Church Divided

*"Every kingdom divided against itself will be ruined,
and every city or household divided against itself
will not stand."*

Matthew 12:25

Recent votes and statements indicate that nearly one-half of the bishops in the United States believe that we should ordain noncelibate homosexuals. The Presiding Bishop of the Episcopal Church agrees and drives that issue on the national scene. They legislate this non-biblical viewpoint with complete disregard for the beliefs of the huge majority of Episcopalians. The surveys of Episcopalians United indicate that as many as 88 percent of the people in the pews oppose the ordination of homosexuals and don't understand how the Church can consider such a move.

The support by many of our Episcopal leaders for the blessing of same-sex unions also flies in the face of scriptural authority and also rejects the opinion of the Episcopal membership.

Thus, using scriptural mandate as our guideline, we are forced to conclude that many of the decisions being made by Episcopal leadership today are invalid and displeasing to God. On the issue of ordaining noncelibate homosexuals and blessing same-sex unions, the Scriptures are clear. These should not even be issues in a Christian denomination. Of course, we believe that compassionate, loving ministry and fellowship can be extended to sinners of all kinds, without in any way blessing or approving of their sin. We recognize that our culture — and at times our Church — has been less than kind and understanding toward homosexuals, and we believe this must cease. But failure to recognize the sin of homosexuals — much less blessing that sin — is neither an act of Christian faith nor an extension of Christian charity.

The problem remains that the Episcopal Church will no longer publicly endorse the Scripture. In 1993, Otis Charles, the retired Bishop of Utah and Dean of Episcopal Divinity School (EDS), announced to his brother and sister bishops that he was a homosexual and had left his wife of 42 years. Rather than meeting this announcement with grief and anguish — that a besetting sin had haunted this poor man for 45 years and finally destroyed his family — most of the public reaction from Episcopalians was supportive, even aggressive: some chided him for not coming out of the closet earlier, while others commended him for his act of courage.

The Episcopal News Service clearly saw an opportunity to make a homosexual hero for the current crusade and produced a glowing feature story about the announcement: "From what Charles said in an interview, it is clear that his highly-developed sense of responsibility to the Diocese of Utah, his family, and ... to E.D.S. prevented him from making a decision to be open earlier in his life. And, he admitted that he had 'internalized' many homophobic stereotypes that constricted his own choices."

The ENS story continued to gush, "Over the years, Charles began to ask what it meant to be a gay man and not respond to that reality, asking if that wasn't a denial of God's intent for his life, a denial of whatever gifts God had given him." No mention here of the numerous biblical mandates which forbid homosexuality and sex of any kind outside of marriage. Rather, our Church's own news service added its voice of congratulation to the bishop for his "courage."

Let us be clear. According to Scripture, walking away from a 42-year marriage — however reluctantly — is neither faithful nor courageous. Disclosing your defeat in a 45-year struggle with homosexuality — but only *after* retiring as a diocesan bishop and seminary dean — is not courage. "Responding to the reality" of one's homosexuality by embracing it and desecrating the sacrament of marriage does not represent a display of the Christian faith.

It is sin.

Bishop Charles' idea that homosexuality was God's gift to him is a sad case of the national Church's desire to mold Scripture to human experience rather than molding human behavior to scriptural guidelines. The bishop confuses the voice of temptation with the voice of God.

The choice — between reconciling one's behavior to one's faith or altering one's faith to fit one's behavior — springs from a conflict that cannot be resolved by human beings alone. In today's Church, two very different perspectives are at work, based on two very different fundamental assumptions: One of those perspectives is moving us toward affirmation of the Scriptures; the other is moving us away from our traditional roots.

On the one hand, the Church has long held to the Fall of Creation as recorded in Scripture, that all people are born "fallen" from a right relationship with God, that we are not at peace with God, that apart from Christ, we strive against God to make our own decisions and do things "our way."

In other words, that we are born in a state of rebellion toward God and sin is natural for us.

We lack the power to change this by ourselves. Our condition is best defined by the words of Saint Paul: The good that I would, I do not; the evil that I would not, I do (Romans 7:19). We are in need of a Savior and Redeemer.

That Savior — the only Savior — is Jesus Christ.

On the other hand, some are convinced that humanity is essentially good — that "if there was a fall, it was upward!" In other words, that we are capable of making our own right choices — and eager to do so. All we need is better education and better living conditions so we can develop to our full potential.

We're not sinners. We're just ignorant!

And all we really need is an *example* to stir our hearts toward "goodness." Jesus Christ was a good example. Nothing more.

Those of the first persuasion believe that life is in large measure a battleground between Good and Evil. We are not ultimately in control of our universe. Since we decide our own fate, we must choose what to believe and who to believe in.

Those of the second persuasion believe that destiny lies largely in the hands of each individual. While there may be external forces to help or hinder, humanity is basically in charge. The formulation of proper human plans and implementation of correct human solutions will one day save the day. Problems usually just require more love or more thought.

Humanity is its own reward, and we can choose from a variety of alternatives to reach our desired goals — analyzing, making and working a plan in a three-step techno-method for success.

A wide chasm stretches between those two perspectives. Neither side will convince the other through intellectual or emotional persuasion. Each belief is deeply and sincerely held. These fundamental assumptions are mutually exclusive, and no amount of "inclusive" language will resolve the differences.

Hurled across the great divide in this debate is the charge that one side or the other *doesn't care about people*. For example, the debate about same-sex unions and the ordination of practicing homosexuals, we are told, is really just about certain people and how much we do or don't care for them.

The clergy who want to endorse homosexuality want to do so out of love and compassion for homosexuals, accommodating them and making them feel valued and welcome in the house of God. It may seem a beautiful, loving attitude to display ... but it is wrong!

Those of us who want instead to help practicing homosexuals to confess and repent of their sins also do so out of love and compassion. We want every lost man and woman to grasp the ultimate love and compassion of Christ by laying down all encumbrances and giving their lives (including their sex lives) to Him.

Both sides care deeply about people and act out of

love for others.

But both sides cannot be correct. The salvation of countless fellow human beings — human beings who remain in the dark, without the light of Christ — is at stake in this debate.

So, too, is the future of our Church.

We cannot deny the seriousness of this issue. Dr. Wolfhart Pannenberg, known to many as one of Germany's most important theologians of the past three decades, has spoken with deep conviction to these issues in a recent essay he wrote and which was translated for publication in the *Church Times* (London-June 21, 1996): "Here lies the boundary of a Christian Church that knows itself to be bound by the authority of Scripture. Those who urge the church to change the norm of its teaching on this matter must know that they are promoting schism. If the church were to let itself be pushed to the point where it ceased to treat homosexual activity as a departure from the biblical norm and recognize homosexual unions as a personal partnership of love equivalent to marriage, such a church would stand no longer on biblical ground, but against the unequivocal witness of Scripture." Pannenberg concludes, "The church that took such a step will thereby cease to be one, holy, catholic, and apostolic."

10 The Courage To Confront

"If your brother sins against you, go and show him his fault, just between the two of you. If he listens to you, you have won your brother over. But if he will not listen, take one or two others along, so that 'every matter may be established by the testimony of two or three witnesses.' If he refuses to listen to them, tell it to the church."

Matthew 18:15-17a

Man is a fallen creature desperately in need of redemption — unable, by design, to save himself. By birth we are all — every one of us — God's fallen children. We are loved but alienated from God our Father. We are brought into fellowship with God only through our relationship to Jesus Christ. This is the essence of the Christian Gospel.

I wish I could rewrite the Bible for the sake of peace between the two sides. But I can't do that, and the truth is that doing so would not bring peace.

For without a life-changing transformation through and in Jesus Christ, we can never know peace.

And the Bible is not mine or yours to rewrite.

I could wish that the exercise of homosexuality,

avarice, gluttony, greed and fornication — to name but a few — weren't defined as sin in the Scripture. Frankly, I can see how some might think this would make being a priest a whole lot easier and a great deal more comfortable. But that list is not ours to revise. Our calling is to share the Christian Gospel — whether popular or not — on Christ's terms.

For those who feel, as I do, that without a bedrock of scriptural authority our faith is weak and ineffective at best, it's little wonder we're experiencing anger and frustration within our beloved Church — that we're so keenly aware of the encroaching darkness. A clergy out of touch with the beliefs of its membership, a Church fragmenting without a consistent message, a leadership that no longer acknowledges the authority of God's Word — these trends in our Church are frustrating indeed.

But there is a better reaction than anger.

There is a call to action which may yet bring about an entirely new Episcopal Church, one devoted to the Scripture and motivated to be a missionary base for hundreds of thousands of Christians dedicated to winning their world to Christ.

It is always darkest before the dawn.

The door that Episcopal leaders have been opening wider and wider — the better to accommodate more and more diverse beliefs — is now open to a degree that would have been inconceivable only a few short years ago. The recent decisions by our leadership regarding homosexuality have opened the door for sin itself to enter the Episcopal Church — and be welcomed. Where will it stop?

The heart of the current Church's problem is that it

is suspending Scripture-based decision making and replacing it with the feel-good theology of a timid Christ who recognizes no sin. That's not Jesus! He was anything but fearful, and when He saw sin, he called it out. "You serpents, you generation of vipers!" Jesus shouted at the Pharisees. Does that sound like a timid man?

And He was speaking to the leaders of the synagogues!

You and I, as believers and joint-heirs with Christ, now have His right to confront the leadership of our beloved Church when we see them in error. It's time for the members of the Episcopal Church to speak out with the words of Christ.

Maybe you fear such a move toward confrontation — perhaps you are afraid that it will be followed by persecution and trials?

It will!

Jesus promised it. He said the meek were blessed, for they would inherit the earth. In that verse, which promises eternal reward, there is also the promise of persecution and trial. The origin of the word "meek" is in a Greek military term that meant to train a horse. The Greeks "meeked" their horses. The man who was going to ride that horse would train it for a year. After a year, the trainer would stand in front of the horse and command it to attention while another man at the horse's side passed a hot iron below its belly. You know, a horse is afraid of fire — and certainly most horses would jump about with that hot iron so near. But if this horse stood at attention throughout the experience, he was considered properly trained and ready for battle. If the horse bolted or reacted in any way, it flunked the meekness test and was destroyed as worthless.

And then Jesus tells us the meek are blessed and will inherit the earth. Jesus is actually saying something like, "Blessed are you when you have been under discipline and stood the test of fire. Then you will inherit the earth." We need to learn that fire is a part of Christian life. God will test us. We are being tested all the time. Being a Christian doesn't mean the Lord will save you from persecution. The Bible *guarantees* that we will be persecuted for His name's sake.

This notion may be difficult to grasp. For me, persecution and trials were a total surprise. I grew up with a good Christian witness around me, and yet I still had the American notion that God somehow counted it a great privilege when I came into the kingdom. I thought He was happy to get me and that He would watch over me and protect me from all harm. When I went into the Church as a priest, I expected everything to be wonderful — and, for the most part, everything was. But nothing prepared me to hit the brick wall I ran into at my third Church, St. George's, San Antonio, Texas.

I went into the position dedicated to working well with the congregation and leadership. I even told the bishop about my dedication and said, "If you ever want my resignation, all you have to do is ask." I could not foresee such an occasion, though, because I had such bright hopes. As a charismatic Episcopalian, I was bursting with excitement and great ideas for how our Church would minister and grow.

In a short while we were growing rapidly and reaching out to our community. However, I didn't take into account how all this hubbub and growth might affect the "old guard" members of the Church, what the logistics of our progress might be — and I stepped on some toes.

After two and a half years, I went to see the bishop about some great new plans I had and a few problems we were experiencing. Instead of sharing my enthusiasm, he asked for my resignation. I never saw it coming, never knew God would let something like that happen to me — not when I believed I was right in the middle of doing His will!

Suddenly, I was out of the job I loved, hard-pressed to provide for my family, faced with how to explain my forced resignation to whatever other churches I applied to. (Most of them, it turned out, didn't want me anyway. Since I came from "that big church," they decided, I probably couldn't meet their needs).

This brought me up hard. I began to wonder what had convinced me that I was exempt from problems and struggles. When had I decided I was the exception to the rule, that God had forbidden fire and hardship to enter my life?

I wanted to be meek — but attaining that meekness meant having to withstand trial by fire. I hadn't prepared myself for that.

Nor have many others in the Church.

Have you?

American Christians grow up with a theology that is largely complacent and apathetic. We do not expect that being a Christian will be difficult. God sovereignly moved in the Episcopal Church to raise up over a million people who received the baptism of the Holy Spirit with the evidence of speaking in tongues, and came into a love of Christ Jesus that they've never known before. When they discovered that they could not be fed quite as easily as they had been before in their churches, when they found that bearing the word of witness was more difficult than they had imagined, when they saw the first sign of tribulation — many of them gave up on their churches or, still worse, on their newfound commitment to Christ.

It is understandable, but it is truly sad. In that particular instance, I have to take my share of responsibility and not just point a finger at those who turned back in the face of persecution. Like many of the leaders and teachers in the charismatic movement, perhaps I failed to prepare people for the way of suffering. I had not suffered much myself and did not help people to be ready for it.

But the fact is: when you follow Jesus, what happened to Him happens to you. Somehow, the Church in America has lost sight of that. In the midst of our praise and raising our hands, we felt the joy — but we forgot the universal significance of the upraised hand. It means surrender. We were telling God that we surrendered our lives to Him, to be used by Him in whatever way He saw fit.

If we had taught that lesson, the Episcopal Church would be a far different place today. Too many of us came into the Church with the expectation of feeding our joy, instead of finding a place where we can serve under fire. And so, at the first sign of fire, many of us bolted.

We avoided teaching the hard word of the cross because in fact we thought it would alienate people. What was the result? People certainly weren't alienated, but they weren't fed, either. The only way to feed the hungry soul is to help it recognize that the way of the cross is the only true way for the Christian.

It's up to you and me to share that message.

That will mean confrontation — perhaps with your own clergy in your own local parish. Confrontation may then lead to persecution — but that's exactly what God intends.

Because of my conservative views and my fervent desire that the Church will turn from liberal ways and come back to the Gospel, I have some detractors. People say to me, "You must be terribly upset by the things people say about you. You are on the Presiding Bishop's hit list." Indeed, many bishops in the Church can't stand the sight of me or the mention of my name.

It doesn't bother me. I don't wear it as a badge of pride, but the truth of the matter is: if nobody's angry with you, then you're probably not doing anything that counts. We have the right to have enemies. Jesus had them, and He expected us to have them. He told us "Love your enemies." That implies He believed we would *have* enemies to love. I'm not chagrined by that or ashamed of it.

If we are in love with Jesus and believe in His cross of salvation, it should be the easiest thing in the world for us to stand up for Him and demand that our Church preach His Gospel. The need to tell our world about Jesus — and to have our Church be the vehicle of that message — ought to burn in our hearts and drive us to take action.

The first thing a new convert wants to do when he finds Jesus is tell somebody else the good news. It's like when you fall in love with your spouse. I've been married for 28 years (and I pray God gives me another 28 with Cherie). Only recently have I really discovered how deep and wide is the patience of this woman, how much she loves me, and how unworthy I really have been to have her. Yet I have never, ever had any difficulties talking about my wife or sharing some of the joy of what it means to be married to her. If that's true for a person in the flesh, how much more it ought to be true of us who have come to know and love Jesus Christ, the one and only Son of God!

I don't know about you, but in my life, Jesus has made all the difference imaginable. What little there is of me worth saving belongs to Christ, and He has saved me. Now, if you can affirm that, you can begin to see that two things need to happen to us as Christians. We need to become bold in our witness and courageous in the faith because once you know the way of the cross is the only way for the Christian — once you've died to yourself, there is nothing left to be afraid of. We certainly do not need to fear the slings and arrows of those within our own Church. It was through my trial in San Antonio that God prepared me to become Executive Director of Episcopalians United.

Yet a spirit of fear pervades the Episcopal Church. Not a fear of God, but a fear of man! The Rt. Rev. Barbara Harris, Suffragan Bishop of Massachusetts, once stood up in a National Church Conference in Kanuga, North Carolina, and made some very derogatory comments about the narrow-mindedness of those of us who believe Christ alone is "the way, the truth and the life." There was little if any Gospel in what she said. Lee Buck, a well-known lay evangelist and an Episcopalian, was on the platform that night. The crowd went wild for Harris' sneering commentary and gave her a standing ovation. Of course, Lee did not rise to honor the incendiary comments, and the man beside him said, "You are really brave." But how much bravery does it take to remain seated when other misguided people stand to honor lies and misrepresentation?

No, it doesn't frighten me to see a crowd of misguided Episcopalians cheering the New Age feel-good religion some of our leadership wants to embrace. What bothers me is that many Episcopal congregations are being taught these lies and falsehoods every week in their parish — and absorb them in silence Sunday after Sunday.

In a North Carolina parish, I witnessed one man in a congregation of about 125 who stood up and said some harsh things — untrue things — in a very confrontational manner. Not one person stood to take the challenge. I believe that man will come back in the self-righteous belief that he has the entire parish on his side, because no one confronted him. No one will follow the biblical command to "speak the truth in love" to him. This kind of timidity — in your heart and in mine — is responsible for the apostate attitudes that now plague our Church. A polite silence pervades our churches which can only be broken by individuals willing to confront half-truths, lies and the misrepresentation of God's Word written.

If your local parish is teaching any other message besides "Jesus Christ and Him crucified" (1 Corinthians 2:2), then you have a problem which needs confrontation. Introducing individuals to Christ Jesus and helping them grow in a relationship with Him is what the Church is all about. The Church ministers in myriad ways, but if we do not introduce individuals to Christ — who alone is both Lord and Savior — we have failed.

We often define our parish identities with statements

that reflect caring communities but are ultimately incomplete:

- "Our Church is a very warm and friendly place."
- "We offer programs to fit the needs of the entire family."
- "We're actively involved in the inner city."
- "We offer Communion to everyone."
- "Our worship services are filled with music and comfort."
- "Our rector is a wonderful person."
- "We served over 6,000 meals to the hungry last year."

Our denomination is in trouble because, to a large extent, we have majored in the minors.

The building can be beautiful, the liturgy well-conducted and pleasantly accompanied by a well-rehearsed, carefully-tended choir. Programs can be well-balanced and equally well-attended. Counseling and pastoral care can provide comfort to individuals in trouble. But if Christ Jesus is not the solid rock of the church's foundation, the parish is built on sand and adds nothing of lasting value to the lives of its people or community.

When the parish no longer cares for its foundation, it becomes not a witness for Christ, but an obstacle in His way. Such a church diverts attention from Christ to people, to buildings, to programs — offering less than faithful alternatives on which to build or rebuild the lives of its members.

But we have the opportunity to take a different direction today.

Did you know that you have a right (and a duty) to stand up in your parish and speak the truth if it's not being proclaimed by the leadership? You can write a letter, or meet with the rector, or organize a committee. You don't have to be timid. If you have died to the world and live to Christ, what do you have to fear?

We need confrontation and trials. Through them come new opportunities for witness and ministry ... and, through them a stronger Christian character is built.

11 Time For Candor

"Speaking the truth in love ..."

Ephesians 4:15

We need to speak the truth — as difficult as it may be — in love. We need to push our clergy and our churches. We don't need to get cynical and threaten to leave, but we need to stand for the truth of the Gospel until it is once again proclaimed in our churches. Your word of witness might well turn a clergyman around.

Sunday after Sunday, as a parish priest, I would have given my right arm to hear just one good, solid comment on the sermon. But that doesn't happen in a receiving line. Whether the sermon was good or bad, dull or exciting, the only thing I heard about it was, "Good sermon, Father." It didn't matter whether I had spent the entire week working on it or had put it together in 25 minutes as I breezed my way from home to Church that morning. Either way, "Good sermon, Father."

Your Parish clergy don't need that. They need to hear truthfully from you if you don't think the sermons are hitting the mark. If you want to change your priest's life as a preacher, give some honest, thoughtful commentary on the sermons in a setting where he or she can listen and respond. And that's not the receiving line!

Call during the week. Make an appointment to discuss the sermon or write a note.

Confrontation in truth helps us all. Being lied to or falsely comforted helps no one. In the long run, false compliments ("Good sermon, Father") assist no one and simply eat away at our souls. There's nothing worse than knowing you've done a bad job and hearing people say, "Good sermon, Father." Did they even listen to it? Are they so used to poor sermons that they really thought this one was good?

When you begin to confront your own Church leadership, I think you might find that they already know the truth. They are simply afraid that someone will call them on it. *Today* is the time for candor — the time to speak the truth in love and encourage your leadership to confront it. Now is the time for true accountability.

The hierarchical structure of our Church, from parish priest to Presiding Bishop, has been built largely on the absence of that accountability. And the result is a clerical structure that is often out of touch with the hearts of the people.

People must begin to ask questions.

We were all stunned to learn that Ellen Cooke, the treasurer of the National Episcopal Church, had swindled us out of millions of dollars. Within a week of her resignation, the staff began finding discrepancies in the various accounts she managed. Now, is it possible that no one noticed until after her resignation what was happening to those funds? That's very unlikely. Someone must have noticed something was going wrong, but everyone was too timid and frightened to say a word. Even when the discrepancies came out, and several of the bishops were aware of it, not a word was mentioned at their meeting in Kanuga. No one wanted the confrontation which would come with that kind of discussion, so it was never addressed until the moment the rest of the world was reading about it in *USA Today.*

Presiding Bishop Edmond Browning highlighted his accountability in this issue, saying, "Ellen had strong support in many quarters, including from the committees she worked most closely with. However, I take full responsibility for hiring Ellen, and keeping her on ... I must bear responsibility for what has happened. The buck stops with me. That's what it means to be Presiding Bishop."

Yet Bishop Browning offers precious little insight into what "taking full responsibility" might mean, other than writing those painful words in *Episcopal Life*. Later in the same column, Bishop Browning offers these self-affirming thoughts: "In sum, what we have learned indicates that, for the most part, our system as conceived was adequate and should have been effective. It is the sad truth that a clever person bent on embezzlement can override the system. The recommendations from Coopers & Lybrand, the independent auditor with expertise in detecting fraud in non-profits, will be used as a basis for tightening our controls."

Do you feel reassured?

The Presiding Bishop's comments failed to explore the real questions of accountability. "What did happen on my watch was a massive betrayal of trust," he wrote. This recalls the passive-language mantra from Watergate and the Iran-Contra scandal: "Mistakes were made." Yes, a betrayal occurred — but a betrayal of *whose* trust, and by *whom?*

Bishop Browning wrote at length about his own sense of betrayal and his personal pain. Does he perceive the more profound pain felt by thousands of Episcopalians whose faithful tithes and offerings were openly squandered for years and years on Mrs. Cooke's penchant for limousine rides and a lifestyle built on wealth that was not her own?

In previous statements, Bishop Browning said that Mrs. Cooke "maintained absolute control of the auditing and reconciliation functions of the Treasurer's office and, for example, prevented others from having access to the Presiding Bishop's discretionary account ledgers. Accordingly, no one on the Treasurer's staff, except Mrs. Cooke, was aware of the activity in these accounts." If this is true, it prompts an obvious question: who gave Mrs. Cooke this absolute control? Ellen Cooke did not function in a vacuum as she methodically embezzled $2.2 million in Church funds from 1990 until her departure in 1995.

Does trust require naiveté or an abdication of a leader's responsibilities? Is it a lack of trust or a spirit of cynicism to ask senior-ranking executives of the national Church to adhere to basic principles of honest accounting? Of course not.

Trust is not a God-given right. Ellen Cooke had no right to our trust. Trust is something we all must earn and maintain. She did neither, yet the Presiding Bishop placed complete trust in her. Trust can be squandered, as the Presiding Bishop squandered ours. I'm sure it caused him great pain.

Accountability recognizes that human beings are vulnerable to sin and erects barriers against temptation. Such barriers would have saved us a horrendous loss and a terrible scandal we didn't need.

Accountability from the Church is your right. God did not say that when you give your money you have to give your brain, too. Rather, He instructed us to be wise as serpents (Matthew 10:16). Push until you get answers. You are to exercise an intelligent, faithful stewardship over the resources God has placed in your hand. He is going to hold you accountable for what you did with the resources (Matthew 25:14ff.), so you certainly must hold the Church accountable when you give.

More than a few dioceses are facing a severe financial crisis. The Episcopal Church Center's budget office now projects a severe shortfall for the years ahead. Dioceses are not able — and some are not willing — to pay their apportionments; parishioners are often either unwilling or unable to pay theirs. We've lost more than a million friends, neighbors and family members from our ranks in the last 25 years.

Part of the problem is that Episcopalians are often asked to give money without full disclosure of how it is spent. That is not good stewardship. Stewardship requires accountability. People are reluctant to give because there is a serious breach in the very fabric of trust we once had in the institution. We've traveled too long without a basic accounting for the actions and the expenditures of our ministries.

We don't ask how our money is being spent. So the money is spent based on the personal perceptions of leadership — perceptions, as we have seen, that are often way out of touch with those of the laity — and the demands of vociferous interest groups.

Have you requested a financial statement from your parish, your diocese or the Episcopal Church Center? Do you know how your offerings are being spent at the parish level? At the diocesan level? At the provincial level? If not, why not?

Would you invest in a corporation that did not disclose its expenditures and activities? Would you invest in a business that did not receive an independent audit each year?

Don't get me wrong. I love our Church.

I want to see it prosper in the faith.

I want to see us grow again.

But for God's sake (and for our own), I believe it is time for candor, honesty and accountability. It would be wrong to view our current financial straits simply as a polite discussion about money. We need to trust each other enough to speak the truth. The Lord wants us to speak the truth in all matters — including money.

But accountability is not always or only about money. Accountability both restores and promotes truth in every area. The Church owes accountability to you in the message it proclaims to the world. Your parish and diocese owe you accountability for staffing and programs.

We don't normally evaluate the ministries of our priests or bishops. As a consequence, we often have no idea what they do or how they go about doing it. They have no concrete ideas as to our desires and needs — yet we blame them for failing to fulfill those unspoken needs.

Does your parish regularly evaluate the work of its clergy? If not, why not?

Is your parish Sunday School instilling your children

with the excitement of Christianity, or does it simply "turn them off" toward religion?

We hear more Scripture on Sunday than any other denomination, yet we remain among the more biblically and theologically illiterate of Christians. Our children grow up, only to leave the fold and wander aimlessly or find spiritual direction in another denomination. Why?

We need a thorough evaluation of everything we do if we are to face the future faithfully. I love the Episcopal Church, and I love the company of Episcopalians. But I love Christ Jesus far more. The Church can never be a substitute for Jesus. The Church that fails to place primary focus on introducing individuals to Him is guilty of making itself an idol.

And idols always have feet of clay.

You have a right to know that your Church is not engaged in idolatry. You can call upon your Church to take sin seriously. Congregations must be taught that sin is real, and dangerous, and that it can not only be repented of and forgiven — but conscientiously avoided in the first place.

We must confront the sins of our leaders — and our own personal sins, as well. If we make excuses for sin — mistaking sentimental tolerance for love — we dishonor Him who died to bear the penalty for sin on the cross.

The measure of sin is not our own experience or inclinations, but the price Jesus Christ paid to save us from it. If He took sin that seriously — if He confronted it at such a deep personal cost to Himself — how can we not face honestly and courageously the terrible choices of our own Church?

12 Why This Hill?

"Does the Lord delight in burnt offerings and sacrifices as much as in obeying the voice of the Lord? To obey is better than sacrifice, and to heed is better than the fat of rams. For rebellion is like the sin of divination, and arrogance like the evil of idolatry. Because you have rejected the word of the Lord, he has rejected you ..."

1 Samuel 15:22-23

Conservatives and traditionalists did not choose to make our stand on the issue of human sexuality. We simply had no choice.

The homosexual activists who demand acceptance while refusing true dialogue about the morality of their behavior have forced us to confront the issue.

The bishops and priests who violate the expressed position of the Church by performing noncelibate homosexual ordinations and blessing same-sex unions have forced us to confront the issue. In asking us to bless the experience of homosexuality, they are demanding that we give assent to a process which must rewrite Scripture and nullify the Word of God. They insist that we disavow almost 4000 years of Judeo-Christian moral teaching — and we cannot.

So the battle is joined.

And since the battle — the battle for the soul of our Church — is being waged on the front of human sexuality, it is there we must make our voices heard. In *The God Who Is There*, Francis Schaeffer quotes Martin Luther as writing:

> If I profess with the loudest voice and clearest exposition every portion of the truth of God, except precisely that little point which the world and the devil are at that moment attacking, I am not confessing Christ, however boldly I may be professing Christ. Where the battle rages, there the loyalty of the soldier is proved, and to be steady on all the battlefield besides is mere flight and disgrace if he flinches at that point.

Frankly, I wish the battle were being waged elsewhere. I'd rather be doing almost anything else. But if the battle is lost here, the war for the soul of the Episcopal Church will be lost.

How has it come to this?

In 1979, twenty bishops — most prominent among them Presiding Bishop Edmond Browning, who was then Bishop of Hawaii — signed a statement dissenting from a General Convention resolution affirming this Church's historic and biblically faithful teaching on human sexuality.

Five General Conventions later, almost half of our bishops now actively support an obdurate homosexual lobby representing less than two to three percent of the Episcopal Church.

What changed? What has happened to our Church during this long, destructive process of debating whether we can change the laws of God regarding homosexuality and other sexual sin?

The *Church* has changed. We have continued our decline in numbers and morale. Church structure desperately needs an overhaul. National and diocesan budgets require repeated cuts. Our clergy display a less concerted vision to reach a broken world with the good news of Jesus Christ.

And we have no clear teaching on human sexuality from the House of Bishops.

In recent years, our revisionist-leaning leadership engineered the dialogues on human sexuality, purportedly to show that Episcopalians were now ready to embrace sins historically believed to be outside the realm of Christian behavior, such as homosexual activity and heterosexual activity for single people. Our own surveys make it clear that most Episcopalians do not believe these lifestyles glorify God or should be condoned by the Church. The sexuality dialogues seemed to indicate the opposite.

From the beginning, the process was severely biased, giving many participants the feeling that the conclusions were preordained. If you heard about or took part in the dialogues in your local parish, you may have felt this way, too. One attorney concluded from his participation that the dialogues were like a skilled cross-examination of a witness: having answered a series of well-formulated questions, the witness is led to draw the conclusion the examining attorney desires to have stated in front of the jury. No other conclusion would be possible.

(You've probably seen this done dozens of times by Perry Mason or Matlock — if you participated in the dialogues, it has now been done to you! Subtly, you have been moved along the road to approval of homosexuality. It was a foregone conclusion.)

It was sad enough that the process was biased and the surveys skewed, but the dialogues were supposed to represent the majority of Episcopalians — while in fact only *one percent* participated. If you didn't participate in the dialogues, your opinion doesn't count.

The voices of the overwhelming majority of sincere, dedicated Church members will never be heard on morality issues such as this if we do not take some action, and quickly. But perhaps you are undecided about these issues yourself.

Fairness and compassion toward homosexuals is a major concern of all parties in the debate — conservatives, moderates and liberals — yet the questions of ordaining practicing homosexuals and blessing same-sex unions are among the most divisive to affect the Episcopal Church in recent years.

The debate has not only become divisive but also confusing, as a small, hard-core group of militant homosexuals and revisionists have sought to dictate legislation and control the dialogue. At the beginning of the debate, they proudly gave us the original Kinsey estimate that 10 percent or more of the population was homosexual. Today, that figure has been proven deliberately misleading. Consistent studies in both Europe and the United States have shown that about 1.8 percent of the population is either homosexual or bisexual with about 1 percent being exclusively homosexual. We are not dealing with a significant minority, but rather a small number of individuals engaged in abnormal behavior.

The argument for the acceptance and approval of homosexual behavior has been at the vortex of what has been termed "the sexual revolution." Biblically and traditionally, sexual intercourse has been limited to the con-

fines of marriage between husband and wife with pro-
creation as its principal purpose and pleasure as secondary. That norm has been heavily challenged by the
media and by some of our Church leaders as they have
sought to portray a culture engaged in rampant sexual
activity and alternative lifestyles.

In the midst of this societal and church-wide dialogue, we were told that 50 percent of U.S. marriages
are headed for divorce. According to *Leadership
Magazine* (Summer, 1996, pg. 69), this dubious statistic
started one year when someone at the Census Bureau
noted that there had been 2.4 million marriages and 1.2
million divorces. Comparing the two figures for that year
alone without taking into account the 54 million existing
marriages, a very quotable — but highly inaccurate —
statistic came into common usage. The truth is that in
any given year only two percent of all married couples
will divorce. According to recent studies covered in
Newsweek (September 30, 1996), the average rate of heterosexual infidelity is 21.2 percent among men and 11.8
percent among women. These facts, while disturbing, do
not indicate the breakdown of marriage or a culture
massively engaged in sexual profligacy.

The facts portray a very different picture from the
one we have been given over the last 20 years. There's
no denying that we are sexual beings. Nor can we deny
that as a culture, our sexual appetites have taken center
stage, being fed and encouraged constantly by an enter-
tainment industry exploiting natural human desire.
However, there is no data to substantiate that errant
behavior is on the increase or that marriage is breaking
down in the face of alternative lifestyles.

There is hope that the Church may yet return to her

right mind in Christ.

The Christian faith has sustained and strengthened us, encouraged and corrected our behavior. The faith "once delivered to the saints" and articulated in the Bible has been under assault but remains true as the Word of God. Neither fornication nor adultery is healthy, normal behavior for Christians (or anyone else for that matter). Their consequence is often tragic and is always sinful.

No. Now is not the time to cave in to those engaged in deviant behavior, to those whose minds and desires have become corrupted by the permissive culture and the temptations of the flesh. Their participation in the life of our faith community has now become corrosive. Having seen the face of the Deceiver, we must stand resolute in the truth of the Gospel.

James 1:3 says that "the testing of your faith develops perseverance." God has permitted a time of testing among us all as Episcopalians in order that we might develop perseverance. The design and purpose of his testing is not so that we might grasp some "new truth" about human sexuality, but rather that we might affirm God's truth in the Bible to the health of our souls and our families.

Acceptance of homosexuality actually threatens the Church's position on Christian marriage — one of the building-blocks of a strong Church and one of the its most important sacraments. Even if our bishops do make the right choice regarding ordination of active homosexuals, we'll still have problems — if they do so without undergirding Christian marriage.

Let's first take a look at what the Scriptures have to say about marriage and why it has always been regarded as a sacrament of our Church.

13 Understanding Christian Marriage

"This is now bone of my bones and flesh of my flesh; she shall be called 'woman,' for she was taken out of man. For this reason a man will leave his father and mother and be united to his wife, and they will become one flesh."

Genesis 2:23, 24

The Celebration and Blessing of a Marriage in *The Book of Common Prayer* opens by defining Christian marriage in terms that distinctly set it apart from a secular union of two individuals:

The bond and covenant of marriage was established by God in creation, and our Lord Jesus Christ adorned this manner of life by His presence and first miracle at a wedding in Cana of Galilee. It signifies to us the mystery of the union between Christ and His Church, and the Holy Scripture commends it to be honored among all people (p.423).

Christ's coming transformed traditional marriage roles of dominance and submission with a new law of love. Although many have misinterpreted the woman's submissive role as slavery or the husband's leadership role as complete dominance, the New Testament gives us a very different description of the love between husband and wife. Ephesians 5:22-30 declares:

> Wives, submit to your husbands as to the Lord. For the husband is the head of the wife as Christ is the head of the church, his body, of which he is the Savior. Now as the church submits to Christ, so also wives should submit to their husbands in everything.
>
> Husbands, love your wives, just as Christ loved the church and gave himself up for her to make her holy, cleansing her by the washing with water through the word, and to present her to himself as a radiant church, without stain or wrinkle or any other blemish, but holy and blameless.
>
> In this same way, husbands ought to love their wives as their own bodies. He who loves his wife loves himself. After all, no one ever hated his own body, but he feeds and cares for it, just as Christ does the church — for we are members of his body.

Wives are to serve in a new way — not out of fear or grudging duty, but "as to the Lord." That means a response of love, joy and delight — out of a desire to please Christ.

Why?

Because He has given His all for us and spared nothing on our behalf.

In turn, the husband is to be the "head" of his wife — in a way so different from male dominance that it is astonishing. Following Christ's example means that a husband is to spare nothing — not even his own life — in his care and concern for his wife. He must think of her as himself, his very own flesh, nourishing and cherishing her as Christ does the Church. Christian marriage is intended for baptized, committed Christians who desire to live a life exemplary of the bond between Christ and His Church.

"In the Lord, ... woman is not independent of man, nor is man of woman," according to 1 Corinthians 11:11. The pattern set forth is not one of dominance and subjection, but rather one of interdependence in a common desire to serve Christ.

First Peter, Chapters 2 and 3 expand the teaching of how Christians are to behave in the world (putting away guile, malice, insincerity, envy and slander, we are to accept Christ's use of us in the building of His temple). This teaching narrows to how marriage should function as well. Wives are to behave in a manner which encourages a husband's commitment to the Lord. A wife is to exhibit reverent, chaste behavior and a gentle, quiet spirit. Husbands are to be considerate of their wives, bestowing honor on them.

Why are wife and husband to act in such a manner? Because through marriage, they have become partners in the work of Christ and in the inheritance of His kingdom (1 Peter 3:7). Failure to act accordingly is a hindrance to prayer and thus breaks communion with God for both parties. A broken or failing partnership is a poor witness to the love of God. Titus 2 brings this teaching to its greatest clarity in discussing righteous behavior when it encourages us to live in such a way that the Word of God may not be discredited (Titus 2:5). The teaching of Colossians 3:12-21 follows the same pattern of giving guidelines for all Christians and then special instructions to husbands and wives:

Therefore, as God's chosen people, holy and dearly loved, clothe yourselves with compassion, kindness, humility, gentleness and patience. Bear with each other and forgive whatever grievances you may have against one another. Forgive as the Lord forgave you.

And over all these virtues put on love, which binds them all together in perfect unity.

Let the peace of Christ rule in your hearts, since as members of one body you were called to peace. And be thankful.

Let the word of Christ dwell in you richly as you teach and admonish one another with all wisdom, and as you sing psalms, hymns and spiritual songs with gratitude in your hearts to God. And whatever you do, whether in word or deed, do it all in the name of the Lord Jesus, giving thanks to God the Father through him.

Wives, submit to your husbands, as is fitting in the Lord. Husbands, love your wives and do not be harsh with them. Children, obey your parents in everything, for this pleases the Lord. Fathers, do not embitter your children, or they will become discouraged.

Who then is the "head" of the marriage? Christ Jesus is rightly the head of a Christian marriage and household. The husband's role is to lead the way to Christ, to point to Him by word and example and to function at all times under the Lordship of Christ and to the glory of God. He is to conduct himself in that leadership of family as Jesus did in training the disciples and still does for us today — teaching, encouraging, correcting, serving and laying his life down for them.

The characteristics of a Christian wife are outlined in Proverbs 31:10-31. Her talents are faithfully utilized to serve her Lord, her husband and her children. "Her husband has full confidence in her" (Proverbs 31:11). She is industrious, strong, and the teaching of kindness is on her lips. She is supportive of her family in the fullest sense of the word. Her husband is honored by her support of his leadership in the home and in the world at large. She does not seek to dominate, but rather takes her direction also from Christ's example (John 13:3-5, 12-17) and exhibits her faith and trust in the Good Shepherd through service.

Thus we see that the biblical teaching on marriage does not indicate a relationship which is fixed or static — with rigid roles, clearly-designated duties and lines between which each partner must stay. Rather, a Christian marriage is to be something alive, exciting and on the move as each spouse shares with the other that "give-and-take" love we see exemplified in Christ. In marriage, the two partners become one — unique and interdependent. Each Christian marriage is different from the others, yet each is called to bear witness to the love of Christ and make Him known.

Sadly, same-sex unions cannot conform to this witness because they have their foundation in practices the Bible clearly defines as sinful.

14 A House Divided

"If we claim to have fellowship with Him yet walk in the darkness, we lie and do not live by the truth. But if we walk in the light, as He is in the light, we have fellowship with one another, and the blood of Jesus, His Son, purifies us from all sin."

1 John 1:6-7

Nowhere in Scripture does the Lord address the blessing of same-sex unions — because homosexuality is soundly rejected as sinful and therefore incapable of fulfilling one of the primary purposes of Christian marriage: to glorify Christ and demonstrate His love.

Among other texts, Paul's words in 1 Corinthians 6:9-10 make it clear that in no way can the Church condone homosexuality: "Do you not know that the wicked will not inherit the kingdom of God? Do not be deceived: Neither the sexually immoral nor idolaters nor adulterers nor male prostitutes nor homosexual offenders nor thieves nor the greedy nor drunkards nor slanderers nor swindlers will inherit the kingdom of God."

We must remember that the Church is not primarily in the business of blessing unions, but of introducing the world to Christ. Christian marriage is to be an example of Christ's love and part of the overall Church's mission. The sin of homosexuality cannot exemplify Christ. Christian marriage is a calling, and in a Christian marriage, God is the third party to this calling. Those who ask us to bless same-sex unions ask God to become a third party to something He has made clear He opposes.

In the same manner, the ordination of homosexuals is anathema to God our Father because He expects His ministers to glorify Him and be an example of His love. A noncelibate homosexual cannot please God. Therefore, God's calling on His people to glorify Christ and allow Christ to live in and through us is denied by the endorsement of homosexuality within the Church.

The homosexual lifestyle denies the primacy of "Christ in you, the hope of glory" (Colossians 1:27) in other ways. David Morrison, a celibate Christian man with a primarily homosexual orientation, writes of his life before Christ, "Being publicly gay, wearing buttons and carrying signs, had been a crucial part of my self-definition since I was 20. My sexual orientation became the most important part of my identity, and I was part of a social movement saying it should be that important ... Being gay means giving oneself over to homosexuality to the point where it becomes a foundation of one's identity, influencing and dominating all other aspects."

Morrison discovered after his conversion that no Christian can define his identity by anything other than Christ. "Eventually all Christians must face Christ's cross in terms of their entire life, sexual orientation and all. If you are active in homosexuality, where have you put your life in relation to that cross? And if Christ is not Lord in your sexual life, where is He Lord?"

The Bible clearly defines any sexual act outside of marriage as sin which — like all sin — results in separation from God. The liberal movement in our Church today would have us accommodate the sin of homosexuality rather than help brothers and sisters to overcome it.

Orthodox Episcopalians face a dual challenge. We must stand with Scripture's consistent teaching that homosexual intercourse is contrary to God's purpose for our sexuality. Yet we must also resist any temptation to hate homosexuals. The debate is not whether homosexuals have a place at the Episcopal table. They have as much of a place as heterosexuals. The debate is about what standards of sexuality the Church will proclaim.

The desire to be loving which the liberal elements of our church show toward homosexuals is to be commended. They fear that the Episcopal Church has become "a place where some members of our Church no longer feel included, where those living in non-traditional relationships might no longer expect to find a place or a welcome in the Body of Christ and where gay and lesbian clergy might question whether or not their gifts are still wanted by the Church they love," according to a statement by Bishop Spong signed by a total of 52 bishops at the 1994 General Convention.

The fear is legitimate, but their answer for it is simply not biblical or acceptable: "... we also believe that those who know themselves to be gay or lesbian persons, and who do not choose to live alone, but forge relationships with partners of their choice that are faithful, monogamous, committed, life-giving and holy are to be honored."

The document continues, "... our lives and our experience as bishops have convinced us that a 'whole' (sic.) example to the flock of Christ does not exclude a person of homosexual orientation nor does it exclude those homosexual persons who choose to live out their sexual orientation in a partnership that is marked by faithfulness and life-giving holiness."

(These bishops once again strike on the theme that human experience is and ought to be as important as Scripture. One of the signers of that statement, Bishop Frank T. Griswold, echoed the supposed primacy of human experience over Scripture when he said he accepted the validity and morality of many sexual alternatives to marriage "based upon my own experience of grace in the lives of persons whose sexual identity has been expressed outside the classical and normative categories.")

There is a better response to Christian brothers and sisters who struggle with the issue of homosexuality than to tell them (untruthfully) that their actions are not sinful. Some Episcopalians believe that the surrounding culture's real sin is hatred of homosexuals, and that the Church should be a refuge for oppressed individuals. These Episcopalians have a point, but they err by insisting the Church can only be a refuge for homosexuals by approving homosexuality. We can provide homosexuals the refuge of a loving God who forgives, and a promise of life eternal if they repent and allow Christ to live in them. This is our message of love to all sinners, including homosexuals (1 Corinthians 13:6).

There is a host of material and counsel available to those seeking understanding, hope, and healing of homosexuality. Some of the more prominent authors in this field are Charles Socarides, M.D., Joseph Nicolosi, Ph.D.,

Leanne Payne and Joe Dallas, to name but a few. Exodus International and Regeneration (in the Episcopal Church) are among the more prominent ministries centered in hope for healing of the homosexual. For anyone seeking to develop further understanding in addition to their compassion, these resources can be of immense help. For the homosexual seeking release or relief from suffering, they are often a lifeline. Collectively, these individuals and ministries show that homosexuality is neither an acceptable nor an alternative lifestyle. There is hope for those who seek release from the suffering that trails in the wake of this sin. This evil can be fought and overcome while maintaining a deep love and respect for the person(s) so afflicted.

It may seem that the only thought conservatives give to our homosexual brothers and sisters is how to prevent them from becoming priests or having their unions blessed by the Church. Some of us have been guilty of focusing on those issues to the exclusion of comforting the suffering, but that is wrong. Some of us feel wrongly accused of "homophobia" because of our convictions.

Compassion is not the exclusive property of any one group or faction at work in the Church. When it is real, it is a gift from the very heart of God. In Jesus, we know the pain of those who feel excluded. That pain is not something abstract to be studied — it is real. The pain felt by fellow Episcopalians — white, black, homosexual, heterosexual, male, female — is not something "out there." Rather, it is *our* pain. All parties who claim to follow Christ must have an openness to the loving compassion of God and through Him to know the pain and joy of brothers and sisters. We must not deal with each other as abstractions, but learn to love one another.

The Church's struggle with this issue continues to divide us. A week before the General Convention of 1994, Bishop Stewart Wood, Jr. (Diocese of Michigan) revived a new and rebellious tradition by ordaining Jennifer Walters, a noncelibate lesbian. (Bishop Ronald Haines of Washington had likewise ordained a lesbian just a week before the previous General Convention in 1991.)

The Episcopal leadership quietly tolerates these ordinations while orthodox Episcopalians sit shocked in their pews as the Episcopal Church blasts away at its own theological foundation. This is an issue of discipline, and the House of Bishops must be willing to discipline its own members who flagrantly violate General Convention resolutions (and biblical standards) dealing with the volatile issues of human sexuality.

Without a willingness to discipline, no substantiative teaching can be established on either side. What is the value of teaching if bishops permit one another to ignore it? What is the value of a community if there are no common expectations of one another?

15 An Exclusive Inclusivity

"Enter through the narrow gate. For wide is the gate and broad is the road that leads to destruction, and many enter through it. But small is the gate and narrow the road that leads to life, and only a few find it."

Matthew 7:13-14

During its interim meeting in September 1995, the House of Bishops overwhelmingly approved a "mind of the House" resolution stating that equal access to ordination for men and women is mandatory throughout the Episcopal Church. This vote sent a disturbing signal that the authority of personal feelings or conscience — which is so adamantly exalted in the matter of ordaining noncelibate homosexuals — may not be extended to four bishops who refuse, for reasons of conscience (and Scripture), to ordain women or recognize them as priests.

One of the supporters of the resolution, Bishop Frank Allan of Atlanta, said, "We can respect one another in our theological differences — but the notion of conscience has all too often been used to circumvent what we believe, and has been used as a cloak to enable individuals to do whatever they think is right in their own eyes."

He makes my point exactly, only he does not want to apply the same rules to those on his liberal side of the fence. Christians' lives are bound by promises. Beginning with baptism, we subordinate the freedom of individual conscience and commit our lives to Jesus Christ as Lord and Savior. In baptism we "die to self" and rise to new life in Him. The Christian Church was not founded on the principle of individual conscience, but on a willingness to subordinate one's conscience to Christ Jesus as He is revealed to us in the Word of God. Bishops and priests take a vow to uphold the doctrine, discipline and worship of the Church. In doing so, they willingly declare the subordination of their will and their personal conscience to the stated beliefs of the Church.

Although I personally support the inclusion of women in the priesthood, I can see that those bishops who do not agree stand on well-tested theological — if politically unstable — grounds. Such is not the case for the proponents of noncelibate homosexuals, yet our leadership will take no stand against it. The words of Bishop Allan could someday justify, during a not-too-distant meeting of the House of Bishops, driving out those of us who oppose the ordination and clerical ministry of noncelibate homosexuals. We stand on long-tested, solid theological ground, but that ground is politically unstable in today's Episcopal Church.

"In those days, Israel had no king: everyone did as he saw fit," Scripture tells us in Judges 17:16. When leaders leave Scripture, tradition and reason in the dust of individual conscience, feeling and experience, then mere political power becomes the arbiter of truth — and truth is the casualty.

At the 1994 Convention, the House of Bishops considered a Pastoral Teaching on Human Sexuality which contained as part of its innocuous introduction, "This Pastoral Teaching then is not intended to offer a particular solution or some new unusual perspective on the issues, nor have we changed the present teaching of the Church on any of these issues." Yet the document went on to declare that sexual relationships reach their fullest potential in lifelong unions between adults, and that "We believe this is as true for homosexual as for heterosexual relationships and that such relationships need and should receive the pastoral care of the Church."

This obvious contradiction to the teaching of the Church was favored by bishops out of touch with the importance of God's Word and with the feelings of the laity. Bishop Orris Walker, Long Island, illustrated this contradiction vividly, saying "Is this Church going to say to them that sexual intimacy for them is abnormal if it does not occur within marriage? If this Church expects me to go back to the streets of Brooklyn and Queens with that one, it ain't going to fly."

The Teaching was altered during the General Convention and later de-emphasized as a Pastoral Study Document rather than a Pastoral Teaching — but even so it is clear that our Church has not resolved the discord surrounding sexuality. Episcopalians live in a time of cognitive dissonance, desperate to reconcile our teaching with the behavior of sinners rather than changing our behavior to be in harmony with Church teaching. Although we have debated the question of homosexuality for over 20 years, some Episcopalians talk as if they are still waiting for the revealed will of God. Such talk assumes God has been silent on the question of sexuality throughout human history or that God's will has, for some reason, suddenly changed. Our leadership ignores the fact that Jesus said, "Heaven and earth will pass away, but my words will never pass away" (Matthew 24:35). God's law does not change, yet Episcopal Church leadership tries to negate it.

The Rev. F. Earle Fox wrote from the 1994 General Convention:

> Committees appointed to examine sexuality issues are almost without exception stacked to exclude fair representation of conservatives. This is not an occasional attitude, but a systematic manipulation of truth and of policy decisions.
>
> People unalterably committed to the so-called liberal viewpoint on human sexuality cannot afford an honest discussion of the facts because the biblical, medical and psychological evidence points clearly toward a sexuality based on life-long, monogamous, heterosexual relations.
>
> Exactly on this issue of due process, the Church is dysfunctional — a dysfunction cleverly fostered by people who know that any open discussion would mean a short end to their sexuality agenda.

Tragically, this is correct. And until theologically conservative Episcopalians are allowed to bring the truth of Scripture to the table for honest debate, we will have neither unity nor progress within the Church. Unity is a gift from God that comes as we practice the truth in following Christ Jesus (Romans 15:5). Defense of that truth requires individual discipline and a willingness for the community to discipline its members. Our leaders aren't willing.

The leadership seems unable to accept that conservative/orthodox Christians revere the truth, the only revealed truth: the truth found in Scripture. For many, the mere word "conservative" conjures up images of wild-eyed, fanatical fundamentalism — a check-your-brain-at-the-door devotion to ancient, musty rites and teachings that no longer fit the temper of the times.

For others (who might actually feel their own sense of allegiance to ancient, musty rites and teachings), "conservative" means a battling politico — one whose only spiritual fulfillment is found in a good scrap ... whose delight is not so much in truth as in a denominational donnybrook on the grandest possible scale.

The stereotypes have grown from two sources: the occasional (and deeply regrettable) personal excesses of those holding to the conservative position, and the deliberate constructions of those who oppose that position.

Some are bewildered by conservatives' love for the truth — but should they construe that love as hatred for anyone who chooses to ignore the truth?

Some may feel convicted by the timeless truth of Scripture and the living examples of tradition — and as a response to that conviction, find themselves portraying those Scriptures as outdated and tradition as dead weight.

Some are intimidated by the clear-eyed convictions and open motives of conservatives — and perhaps they instinctively attempt to disguise them as "wild-eyed" and "closed-minded."

Some are, regrettably, enmeshed in apostasy — and they strive to redefine that apostasy as "tolerance."

Yet what does their idea of tolerance come to when

some liberals are willing to see this Church torn apart for the sake of a worldview that makes truth relative and encourages sin? For some members of the liberal movement, the departure of orthodox Episcopalians is a goal. Barbara Harris, for instance, teaches inclusivity through exclusivity. She has urged liberals to declare themselves the traditionalists of the Church because they are faithful to the "traditional teaching of the inclusivity of the Gospel ... If this means saying goodbye to the selective traditionalists in our Church" and others in similar denominations, Harris says, then they must "say enough is enough ... and goodbye."

This exclusive "inclusivity" Bishop Harris and other liberals call for has proven disastrous for the Episcopal Church. On the surface, the notion of wanting to embrace everyone and include them uncritically in the life of the Church seems a noble and warmly human aspiration. This kind of thinking involves a constant reiteration of the mercy of God and of the commandment to "Love one another." It commends in theological terms a psychological approach popularized by Carl Rogers and known as "unconditional positive regard."

Jesus said, "Do not judge, or you too will be judged" (Matthew 7:1). Those who build their theology on the notion of inclusivity find in these words an injunction to stop talking about judgment in matters both ethical and theological. They refuse to recognize that we will be judged by the same standards by which we judge.

Through an inclusive theology, God becomes a *laissez faire* Father who loves everyone and expects nothing personally from anyone. We're all God's children and He uncritically accepts us all, just as we are. You have read in these pages how such a "theological" understanding affects us as Episcopalians. There were waves of public anger in 1989 when Bishop Spong ordained a noncelibate homosexual to the priesthood to demonstrate his "inclusive" theology. Only seven short years later, with inclusivity now ingrained, the Court for the Trial of a Bishop decided that no doctrine or canon law forbade a similar ordination.

Episcopal structures can take a fringe idea (like condoning homosexuality) and quickly turn it into accepted policy. Any number of liberal clergy call this "incarnational theology" — acting first, then creating their theology later, based on their subjective experiences and all-important feelings. Feelings and subjective experience are the touchstones of inclusive theology. No rules, no judge — no accountability.

Each person is left free to work out his own salvation based on his own feelings and perceptions — with the idea that we are all basically good, and (given the right environment and wise social institutions) we will all be loving and behave beautifully. The doctrine leads us to believe that no one would ever willingly do anything wrong if only the system were right (although advocates of this view are always a little vague on how we are supposed to define right and wrong). Most importantly, no one is *ever* at fault.

This inclusive theology is what it sounds like: a marvelous fantasy generated by the irresponsible child within and appealing to the self-indulgence and narcissism that resides in us all. The "inner child" in me wants desperately to believe that self-indulgence is the path to true enlightenment and a good society. But, in spite of my best efforts at denial and self-delusion, this simply does not square with the evidence that 50 years of living has placed in my path — nor with the biblical mandates of Holy Scripture.

Though it begins with good intentions, the inclusivity theology brings not utopia but a highly chaotic world in which the conflicting feelings and personal desires of various persons and groups can only be resolved by the exercise of power. People need rules — and yes, need, from time to time, to be judged. Hopefully, those rules will be tempered by mercy — but they must exist. How cruel it would have been for God to create a human society that left us in the dark as to our purpose — and without rules and guidelines to show us how to function to the best advantage for ourselves and others.

Yet this is what inclusivity implies — a world without rules and with no apparatus for making them other than one's own subjective experiences and feelings. The spirit of inclusivity is captured very well in a quote from Andrew Getman, a young man who attended a conference sponsored by the National Church and decided: "Truth is in the darkness and in the light, and it does not see a difference."

The problem with this warm and sentimental theology is that — out of the best intentions — it leaves us in the chaos of our own feelings and desires. In seeking to elevate the person who feels disenfranchised, it abandons God and the Bible through which He has spoken. Scripture implores us, "Trust in the Lord with all your heart and lean not on your own understanding; in all your ways acknowledge Him, and He will make your paths straight" (Proverbs 3:5-6).

This last decade or so of Episcopal life is, in many ways, a lot like all the others — a record of limited successes, human failings, institutional ineptitude, and an avalanche of words, not all of them faithful. But, in another sense, this past decade *is* radically different from those of years past. Laboring under a false theology of inclusivity, we have sought to *exclude* the God Who speaks to us in Scripture.

The Episcopal leadership we've chosen has undermined the rules and expectations God so lovingly revealed. In the process, our Church — which should be God's light in the world — has done what the human heart left to its own devices so often does, increased the darkness.

The desire to include everyone in my church is a nice sentiment. The problem is: it isn't "my" church. It's Christ's. He has made it clear that the price of following Him is to repent of the things which offend God. To do less may indeed include us in a human institution, but that institution will not be His Church.

"Let us run with perseverance the race marked out for us..."

16 Divorce Is Not The Answer

"If we are faithless, He will remain faithful, for He cannot disown Himself."

2 Timothy 2:13

At one point in my marriage, I knew I had every right to leave my wife. I could have sat down at that point and listed objectively every reason for going, and known with absolute certainty that she wouldn't miss me if I did. In fact, when it came down to it, only one thing kept me from leaving in those difficult days.

I had stood before an altar and vowed I wouldn't.

I wasn't born in the Episcopal Church. I made a conscious decision as an adult to join this fellowship. In fact, my wife and I met in an adult confirmation class and were confirmed the day after our marriage. And, just as I could during those rocky times in my marriage, I can sit down today and list every objective reason why I have a right to leave this Church.

Only one thing keeps me here.

I stood before a group of bishops, clergy and laymen and said, in effect:

"I am duty-bound and honor-bound to serve this

Church. Although she would leave me, I will endeavor not to leave her."

You made a similar vow when you were confirmed.

Is divorce the answer?

Should we give up and leave the Episcopal Church? Certainly many say it is too far gone down the path of liberalism and relativism to save. The question becomes whether to leave for greener pastures — to create a new denomination for the conservative and moderate Episcopalians who would be willing to splinter from the Church — or whether to stay and strive within the Church, not just for reform, but for a whole new Church, inside and out.

The first place to look for the answer to this question is to God the Father.

What is God asking you to do?

In an earlier chapter, I shared with you my experience of renewal — the one that changed my whole life. But that change came a long while before my wife enjoyed a similar experience and came to know Christ as I did, which was my will for her life. My marriage was fragmenting, and I sought God about which direction to go. Somehow, His work in my life seemed to have alienated my wife.

"Why doesn't she love You like I love You?" I cried out to God.

God's answer was *not* to leave her and move on to someone who did love Him the same way I did.

God's answer was for me to love my wife the way He loved her.

If you are wondering and praying about why your Church doesn't seem to love God the way you love Him, what answer are you receiving from the Father?

Perhaps He is trying to tell you to love this Church the way He loves her.

The choice of whether to stay or go belongs to each individual — but one must make an informed choice. Please be sure you hear from God before you make that decision. It is possible that God may say, "Yes!" to your desire to leave. But until that time comes, stand and fight for the faith once delivered to the saints.

First, bear in mind that if you and I cut and run from the Episcopal Church, leaving the liberals to themselves, it's almost certain that American Anglicanism will die. Given the current erosion and destruction of all the foundations of our faith, it is naive to think that the Episcopal Church of the future will resemble our parent Church of England in any way — except perhaps the form of our services and (in some cases) the architecture.

The Episcopal Church was birthed as the Anglican Church of America. Shortly after the Revolutionary War, it became a national phenomenon. The 39 Articles represent one of the most succinct definitions of orthodoxy in the West, a definition which has held down through the centuries. Our Church is the heir of Anglican tradition in the U.S. It is widely perceived as the closest thing we have to a "national" Church.

If moderates and conservatives leave the Church rather than uniting to save it, America loses the great tradition of Anglicanism, as the Episcopal Church ceases to be a Christian Church and instead becomes — in the hands of liberals and revisionists — a reflection of the popular culture. What a shame for our nation to lose this rich history of faith and tradition!

Moreover, what a shame for you and me and our

families to lose the unique opportunities for spiritual growth which lie ahead for those Episcopalians who stay the course.

It's true we are living through a difficult time in the Episcopal Church, a God-ordained time, when people must clearly choose. God is asking, "Are you for me or against me?" This time is a trial for all of us, and we will only live through it with a reliance on faith, grace and compassion. This is a God-ordained time for a shaking in the household of faith. We have choices to make, and they are not easy choices.

God is raising up a people called to be a living symbol of His loving discipline in the life of His people. This is one reason we are being required to exercise choice about doctrine that 25 years ago no one would seriously have questioned.

- Is Jesus Christ the way, the truth and the life — or is He *a* way, *a* truth and *a* life?
- Is the Bible the Word of God written, or is it simply one among many religious books that speaks of truth, but does not speak *the* truth?
- Does the indwelling life of Jesus Christ, through the power of the Holy Spirit, transform the life of a person committed to follow Him?
- Does the Bible speak of the revelation of God as being absolute, or is His Word relative — applicable to the generations to whom it was first written, but changing with the culture over the course of time?

People will still be struggling with those questions in the next generation. In fact, following Christ will probably be more difficult for your children than it was for you. We are experiencing the end of Western Christendom — of the idea that Christianity, as part of our American heritage, is to be received without much question as a part of our citizenship. That time no longer exists, and soon the whole idea of exercising faith within Western civilization will be much more difficult.

I think that's why we're in a time of testing right now. God is asking us to do something that most of us cannot really remember having to do in our lifetime, and that is to really examine our faith — and be responsible for giving a witness to it.

It was in a remarkably similar time that Elijah said to Ahab, "I have not made trouble for Israel. But you and your father's family have. You have abandoned the Lord's commands and have followed the Baals." He went before the people and said, "How long will you waver between two opinions? If the Lord is God, follow Him; but if Baal is God, follow him" (1 Kings 18:21).

In the Episcopal Church, that time of choosing has finally come. Legislative attacks and counterattacks have revealed the sides in this great battle — a battle into which we have been swept against our will. The battle cannot be avoided. Nor — as past skirmishes clearly demonstrate — can we engage it decisively at the national level. It is fast coming down to what it really always was: you and me. The battle must be engaged in the heart and mind of every Episcopalian as we each take our part in the age-long dialogue with God.

Truth rests solely and solidly on God's side. It always has.

Long ago another man stood squarely and confidently before his people and spoke these words:

Now fear the Lord and serve Him with all faithfulness. Throw away the gods your forefathers worshiped beyond the River and in Egypt, and serve the Lord. But if serving the Lord seems undesirable to you, then choose for yourselves this day whom you will serve, whether the gods your forefathers served beyond the River, or the gods of the Amorites, in whose land you are living. But as for me and my household, we will serve the Lord.

Joshua 24:14-15

Just such a time of choosing is here now.

Will you serve God, who has chosen to reveal unwavering truth? Or will you serve some other god — a god whose truth changes with every whim of human emotion? The answer is not one of passing significance; it is fraught with eternal consequence. All other questions are secondary. God has drawn the line, and each of us must choose — this day — whom we will serve.

If we choose to stand with God, we will be called upon to give witness to the basic Christian teaching that has marked the faith through century after century — and sometimes to speak a hard word to both our Church and culture. And, when we're called on to speak that hard word, it must not be spoken in the abstract. We will speak it to people with faces and names — often people whom we love.

Conservatives are going to have to confront head-on the onslaught of secularism within the Church. It is not going to be comfortable, and it is not going to be easy. People are going to be hurt. For priests, career paths may have to be surrendered.

It is going to be a very difficult time for the Church.

But I cannot believe the *only* future available to the

Episcopal Church is to flounder on the rocky shore.

If you have reached a point in your own personal walk where you really believe the Episcopal Church has no future, then you need to prayerfully consider leaving. Otherwise you may stay only to become some kind of self-fulfilling prophet.

If you feel, like many conservatives I know, that you cannot in good conscience bring the lost into the Episcopal Church for evangelism and discipleship, and if you feel that God has called you to another denomination where His Word is clearly preached and practiced, then it may be time to leave. (To refuse to leave under any circumstances is a form of idolatry.)

But please keep in mind: if you are leaving the Episcopal Church for any other reason except God's clear direction, your "escape" may not be as comforting as you think it will be. Do you really believe there'll be no conflict in your next church? Do you really believe there'll be no challenges to your faith in that church? When those challenges come, will you desert that church and move on to the next one?

Remember: conflict is a part of life, and you will find it no matter which denomination you switch to. Many Americans who grew up during the 1960's and 1970's tend to see conflict and confrontation as areas to be avoided. When they arise, we move on. But that is a very "frontier" style of churchmanship — moving on to the next frontier whenever the established landscape begins to threaten you, or bore you, or confront you. Eventually, you are going to run out of frontiers.

Other denominations are not necessarily less chaotic than our own, as you will discover if you choose to depart. It just happens that our denomination is in the news; our choices are consistently publicized and given a significance that far outweighs our numbers. The reason that our Church has appeared at the center of Christianity for the past several centuries is that we are the nexus of Catholicism and Protestantism, combining the best points of the Roman Catholic Church and the Reformation. Issues that engage us also engage both Catholic and Protestant denominations. Thus the media use us for a gauge of what is happening in Christendom. The issues dividing the Episcopal Church are dividing most other churches, too.

So it appears that American Christians have run out of running space. There's nowhere you can go to avoid trial and persecution: the necessity of being a Christian amid difficult circumstances. In fact, the discomfort we feel now as we try to portray Christ to our world may simply be a preparation for even harder times to come.

Thus it seems to me that — unless you sense a direct calling from God — leaving the Episcopal Church is not the answer to our current struggles. The history of the Christian Church records many circumstances much darker than those we see now in the Episcopal Church. God has never abandoned His Church. Apostasy has been the rule of the day for hundreds of years in the history of the Church, yet God has never let the apostates win out. A branch of the Church may separate itself through apostasy and in time wither and die, but the Church of Jesus Christ moves on.

Remember, the darker it is, the easier it is to see the light!

What of the idea that the conservatives and moderates could walk out of the Episcopal Church, forming a new Church without our liberal brethren? It has been done before. But the history of splinter groups of the Episcopal Church is not particularly fruitful. They tend not only to splinter away from the Episcopal Church, but also from themselves. The Reformed Episcopal Church, for instance — a major attempt by 19th century evangelicals to establish a reformed denomination — came to very little. Most reform movements which step outside the Episcopal Church seem to be birthed amid a lot of talk about the drawbacks of the current Church — but when the time for departure actually comes, very few make the move and support the new entity.

And even if we *were* to try to launch a new Church, think of the lost souls we would be abandoning in the current Church. Our Episcopal brothers and sisters have the witness of Scripture and a long-standing tradition of Christianity placed before them every week — although by and large they have not incorporated it into their lives. It would be difficult for me to say that our grievances with the Episcopal Church were worth more than those souls.

The Episcopal Church today is nearing the breaking point — and that breakdown will leave these non-believing churchgoers even more open to the message of the Gospel. When a denomination like ours — having already lost more than a million members — continues dysfunctionally to confront issues which defy the traditional teaching, our struggle becomes more and more apparent. When a large number of our clergy are active homosexuals, when the sole message of a number of our feminist clergy seems to be women's rights (and their only passion seems to be anger), then the breaking point must be at hand.

What the non-believing clergy are perpetrating on

the Church will have incredibly sad implications for the institution and for the people in the pews. But this very brokenness will open hearts to God. What a shame it would be, at this most important time for evangelism, if those of us who know and truly believe the truth had already abandoned our Church.

The Episcopal Church today is itself a mission field — one far different from the foreign field, and perhaps harder to reach at this moment. But it is made up of people very familiar to us, people we can talk to, people whose foibles and idiosyncrasies we share. We understand these lost souls as perhaps no one else does, and we are better equipped than anyone else to bring them into fellowship with Christ. Can we in good conscience leave the Church — and this mission field — to the self-destructive guidance of the current liberal leadership?

Replacing a lost Episcopal Church with one of my own making will not lead those souls to Christ.

And besides: I know I can never really depart the company of sinners as long as I take myself with me.

Thus we see that the roads of joining or establishing a different denomination are probably closed to us, for they are not likely to bear much fruit. The better course for most of us seems to be remaining within the Church.

Of course, the consequences of staying — even when the national leadership seems to be taking an anti-biblical stance — cannot be avoided. It troubles me a great deal that our leadership seems intent on taking a secular stand on sexual issues — but I am clear on where I stand, and my conscience is clear before God. Does my remaining in the Episcopal Church somehow make me responsible for the sins of my brothers?

No.

Do I feel dirtied by the actions of my Church?

No.

Do I grieve over them?

Yes.

Am I willing to stand and bear the consequences with them?

Yes — because I believe God has called me and you to be the conscience for our Church in this hour, to stand beside the leadership and to call them back to the way of repentance and salvation.

Our brothers have done things we're not proud of, but does that give us the right to abandon them? At various points in all our lives, we have each engaged in reprehensible behavior. But God leads us out of those sins into forgiveness and on to better places down the road. I believe the Episcopal Church, too, will come out to a better place down the road — and what's more, history demonstrates this.

For one thing, the current liberal leadership simply cannot maintain the contrariness they are showing toward God and His Word right now. (I say contrariness because it seems to me that our leadership is intent on choosing the opposite course from whatever the Bible says and whatever Christian tradition dictates. If they carry this to its logical conclusion, soon they won't have a church, but a social club — or, more likely, an anti-social club.) This constant choosing of the anti-biblical stance — demonstrated in areas as diverse as human sexuality and overseas missions — will exhaust itself in time. Those of us who hold firm for the truth will remain a testimony to the great wisdom of Christian history — that standing and bearing witness in the face of apostasy is worthwhile and honored by God.

During these difficult days, ours is a renewed call to bear witness to the truth and to persevere in that witness. We are not called to abandon the Church because there is conflict. Ample conflict troubled the early Church, too. Acts 20:30 underscores a theme prevalent in the New Testament witness, "Even from your own number men will arise and distort the truth in order to draw away disciples after them."

I'm reminded of the story Chuck Colson of Prison Fellowship told about the events in Timisoara, Romania, in December, 1989 — events that sparked the overthrow of the communist government:

It seems a reformed pastor, Lazlo Tokes, was preaching the Gospel week after week and drawing huge crowds. Time and again the government's secret police harassed the clergyman and tried to shut the church down, but Tokes continued to preach. People continued to rally around him.

In fact, the persecution became so obvious that one day the entire square in front of Tokes' church was filled with believers who had come to show their support — Orthodox Christians, Baptists, Catholics, his own congregation.

The demonstration drew government troops to contain the crowd. In this tense moment, a 23-year-old man reached inside his jacket for something he held under his coat. His pastor, beside him in the crowd, quickly said, "No. No weapons."

But when the young man opened his coat, he had only a box of candles. "I just want to light a candle," he said. He lit a candle and passed the flame along — soon the entire square was glowing in candle-light as the crowd sang hymns together.

The government authorities tried to disperse the crowd, but when they wouldn't go, the troops opened fire. The young man picked up a little girl in an attempt to carry her to safety, but he was shot in the leg. When he awakened in the hospital the next day, he found doctors had been forced to amputate his injured leg. His pastor came to visit and console him.

But the young man said, "That's all right, pastor. I lighted the first candle."

Although the forces arrayed against us may seem dark, foreboding, overwhelming, to bear witness to the truth in the midst of the confusion which engulfs our Church today is the challenge set before us — a challenge we cannot deny. For the sake of our children, fellow citizens, and for the sake of our own souls, we dare not be less than faithful.

"Let us run with perseverance the race marked out for us" (Hebrews 12:1). Together, let us continue to light many candles which illuminate God's Word to His people.

17 If Divorce Is Not The Answer, What Is?

"Anyone who listens to the word but does not do what it says is like a man who looks at his face in a mirror and, after looking at himself, goes away and immediately forgets what he looks like. But the man who looks intently into the perfect law that gives freedom, and continues to do this, not forgetting what he has heard, but doing it — he will be blessed in what he does."

James 1:23-25

I once spent a night in a hotel where two high-school proms were being celebrated. A number of young people had rented the room on one side of me and were having a stomping good time inside. In the room on the other side, a woman was complaining at the top of her voice about the party on the other side of my room. She kept calling security, and I spent most of the hours between 11 p.m. and 3 a.m. listening to the guards bang on *my* door.

I think my situation that night is not unlike the situation in the Church today.

On one side of us, we have a group of rather rowdy people who cannot seem to contain their passions, and on the other side we have a group very irate about the wild actions of the others. There we are, huddled under the covers, just trying to get on with our lives, knowing we have just a few hours before we must arise and take on the tasks God has set before us. It looks like the parties in the rooms on each side of us may never be reconciled. But if divorce is not the answer, what is?

"I solemnly declare that I do believe the Holy Scriptures of the Old and New Testaments to be the Word of God, and to contain all things necessary to salvation; and I do solemnly engage to conform to the doctrine, discipline, and worship of the Episcopal Church" (*The Book of Common Prayer,* pgs. 526, 538, 513).

Every deacon, priest and bishop of our Church takes this vow. In the case of bishops, this pledge is made three times — publicly. But many Episcopal clergy, in spite of that vow, don't wish to conform to the Church's doctrine and discipline. Their failure to honor vows, taken in the presence of witnesses, is adulterous (Jeremiah 23:14, James 4:1-4). They commit the very sin they condone.

But they aren't the ones talking about divorce. We are.

The liberals and revisionists are not despairing, throwing up their hands, declaring that they cannot continue in this Church. The conservatives are the ones who fantasize of a new Episcopal Church without "inclusivity" or "incarnational theology." There may be a reason for this. Have you noticed that the partner who wants the divorce is usually the one who refuses to make positive changes to save the relationship?

The liberals of our Church are the activists. They rush ahead of the tide and make things happen, while we conservatives seem united only in our disapproval — and our complete inability to get anything done. Our liberal brothers and sisters don't spend a lot of time on theology, but they do get things done. They don't need to talk about divorce; right now the relationship is going their way.

Three attitudes now prevail in our life as Episcopalians:

- *Liberals/revisionists* say "Do it first — think about it later." That's how they can develop rites for blessing same-sex unions and permitting their use before the Church has done her theological homework or completed her dialogue.

- *Moderates* appear titillated by the actions of the left — and almost persuaded by the thinking of the right — but want to keep all their options open. Moderate bishops at the 1994 General Convention, for instance, refused to sign either an affirmation of the Church's traditional teaching on sexuality or a dissent written by Bishop Spong.

- *Timid orthodox/conservatives* say, "Let's reiterate the truth — but any action would be precipitous." A recent example: a statement of the Irenaeus Fellowship of Bishops that delineated beliefs, but failed to recommend any course of action.

The orthodox can no longer afford to pretend the Episcopal Church is healthy just because their diocese is healthy. As Fr. Richard Kim of Detroit said, "It's time for us to stop complaining and start doing something."

If we want to reform and renew the Church, conservative and orthodox Episcopalians must plant their feet somewhere and take a stand. We cannot achieve unity when we do not honor truth or hold one another accountable. Moderates, too, will have little to offer as long as they twist in the wind, unwilling to discipline a permissive heart with a Christian mind.

Admittedly, we cannot uphold or defend the Episcopal Church as it now exists. Instead, we must defend the Gospel of Jesus Christ within the Church. This is where we should spend our time, energy and resources: not just on the defensive, but with the collective understanding that *a faithful witness is the best offense.* This crisis presents all Episcopalians with a glorious possibility — the possibility that an unfaithful Episcopal Church is dying, and a new, more fruitful Church is about to be born.

For that tremendous transformation to happen, though, we must take the constructive actions necessary to bring it about. If we want to fall in love all over again — with the Lord and with each other — we're going to have to take the plunge.

Let's not be the partner who talks about divorce but refuses to do anything to prevent it. We know divorce is not the answer, so let's go to work — saving the relationship, bringing about a rebirth in our Church, glorifying God and bringing the lost into His kingdom.

Of course, I can't work on the marriage if I'm not willing to work on myself first.

Each of us must realize that we can no longer rely on anyone else to live our faith for us. The "professional Christians" we've hired to do the job — priests and bishops — have either failed or been unable to fulfill the whole calling of God on their own. Many of them don't even believe in the same Gospel we do; many aren't striving toward the same goal of bringing the lost to

Christ. Yes, we commissioned them to do so — but many no longer have the beliefs we want them to uphold.

As you have read, many clergy are far out of touch with the believers in the pews. They cannot effectively do the work of the Church if they don't believe in it. For too long, we have relied on these men and women to carry the burden of missions and evangelism for us. We have separated ourselves from the witness and the proclamation of the Gospel. Our first task, then, is relearning the Christian faith and developing an effective Christian witness.

Christianity is not first a religion. It is a personal relationship with God, a conscious decision to walk with Christ Jesus on a daily basis. For many Episcopalians, though, Christianity is only a religion, and they attend church only as a matter of course. God and His Church have never really become a part of their lives. For these Episcopalians and the other lost souls of world, we must be sure that we understand — and can communicate — what it means to have a relationship with Christ.

18 Developing A Deeper Faith

"I pray that out of His glorious riches He may strengthen you with power through His Spirit in your inner being, so that Christ may dwell in your hearts through faith. And I pray that you, being rooted and established in love, may have power, together with all the saints, to grasp how wide and long and high and deep is the love of Christ."

Ephesians 3:16-18

I'm often asked, "How can I have a relationship with the Lord?" or "How can I find peace?" All such questions derive from our human need to know God. Healthy, lasting and satisfying relationships require effort and time to develop. They don't happen overnight. The following are four steps I commend to you for beginning and establishing (or refining) your own relationship with the Lord — and for sharing with others about how to develop this kind of relationship.

Step One. You have a need for God. Recognition of this need is the beginning of your relationship with the living God. Matthew 5:3 declares, Blessed are those who know their need for God, for theirs is the kingdom of God. If you do not recognize your need for God, you will never know Him: He may be a comforting thought, a final arbitrator or provider of some means to explain the deep questions of life, but for you He will never be a Person who loves and desires to be known by you.

Step Two. You must be willing to devote time and energy to your relationship with God for it to develop and mature. The time-tested ways you can do this are:

- Be attentive to those whom you believe know God. Receive teaching and counsel from those in fellowship with God.
- Make a conscious decision to surrender your life to the leadership of Christ Jesus and then tell at least two other people you have done so.
- Spend time in worship, both personal and corporate. Learn to fully appreciate and honor God's presence.
- Become familiar with God's story by regularly reading His written Word (Hebrews 1:1-2 and Psalm 119:89-96 point out the importance of study).
- Become sensitive to the environment in which your relationship is developing. God is sovereign and His presence (or lack of it) can often be known through the circumstances of our lives.
- Prayer, both personal and in a small circle of Christian friends, must become a regular discipline if your life is to reflect the character of God.

Step Three. You need to know the will of God. If you would know God, you must be open to Him as He is. John 14:6 tells us that Jesus is "the way, the truth and the life" — and that no one comes to God, the Father, except through Jesus. Once you recognize your need of God, the lordship of Jesus in your life becomes your only means of finding the heart of God.

Even Jesus admitted that to hear from God, He first had to be willing to listen. "By myself I can do nothing," Jesus said in John 5:30, "I seek not to please myself but Him who sent me." Jesus knew the Scriptures. Search for God's direction in them, then be willing to do God's will.

Step Four. Experiencing God involves a willingness to change and grow in new ways. Putting God's will into practice, in spite of your feelings, will grow your faith. God promises you peace, but He will work against anything which would encourage you to return to things which dishonor His presence. Jesus promised us abundant life, but this reward only comes as we grow deeper and deeper in relationship with Him. John 14:15 equates love with obedience to His will.

Remember that — despite popular wisdom — seeing doesn't produce belief. On the contrary, belief is what enables us to see God. Likewise, abundant living doesn't produce belief, but believing in and living for God enables us to receive abundant life. The disciple Thomas exemplifies the doubting, skeptical spirit of our age. Happily his story doesn't end with his doubts, but with his falling at Jesus' feet to proclaim, "My Lord and my God!"

The Lord is at least as much interested in you as He is in your "religion." To make the Episcopal Church more than a denomination or a religious affiliation, each of us individually must grasp the life in Christ offered to us. We must make it more than a religion — we must make it a living, growing relationship with God.

We must also become much more aware of the Prayer Book. We must learn what's between those dusty covers besides the Sunday liturgy. I am surprised as I go to gatherings all over the country to hear priests stand up and say, "We're a Church that's proud of the fact that we don't really have any theological statements." I have to wonder: where did this person grow up? Where did he go to school?

We have a Catechism. We have the 39 Articles. We have the Creeds. We have the Bible — all rich with the authority that undergirds our heritage and tradition.

Because of our unique ecclesiastical position — reconciling the Protestant and Catholic traditions — we have been the Church of middle ground in the exercise of faith. This does not mean we have to be smack in the middle of every theological debate. It does not mean that we are bound to embrace both sides of any particular question. It means that, given the parameters of the faith, our theology is squarely down the middle.

For instance, a Christian should affirm Jesus Christ as Lord and Savior, affirming both His divinity and His humanity. We're not allowed to *choose* whether Jesus was human or divine, for the Scriptures clearly tell us He was both. Within the parameters of orthodox Christianity, that's pretty middle-line theology.

But then Episcopalians are historically mainstream Christians. True, we examine the faith. We give ourselves freedom to discuss any issue in the parish. The Episcopal Church I knew in the 1950's and early 1960's discussed political questions as freely as theological ones. Indeed, we *discussed* a wide range of subjects, but what we were *taught* was the faith contained in the Prayer Book and the Scriptures. Our leaders were not free to teach anything they chose. Deacons, priests and bishops were under authority — people with a responsibility to teach as Gospel only what was clearly delineated in the Prayer Book and the Scriptures. Doubts are all right, and questions are to be encouraged — but no one should be free to teach that which is contrary to the Word of God written, or the faith clearly defined in our doctrine, discipline and worship.

But how are you going to know if your priest is teaching sound doctrine or his own ideas if you don't know yourself what is in the Prayer Book and the Scriptures? The Catechism is not there just for you to learn at Confirmation. It is there to instruct you in the faith throughout your lifelong journey. The Catechism defines the true center line, the *via media* so many Church leaders claim they are trying to walk. To actually walk that middle way is to walk with the Catechism and the other historical documents as they're defined for us and to walk according to the Word of God written.

You cannot help but become a better Christian and a better Episcopalian by knowing and understanding the Scriptures. God's Word is not an abstract concept for conforming our lives — it is the mind of God written directly to you; it is your story in God's kingdom, a record of the things God has done for His people and the things He will do for us.

I believe the Episcopal Church is becoming a place where Christians cannot survive spiritually without the power of God in their lives. To experience that power you must first commit your life to Christ and then read and study God's Word as His loving instructions to you as His disciple. Do so, and the Scriptures will come alive to you in a new way, and so will the Episcopal Church.

And, as the Bible becomes foundational for you, you will discover something else. You will discover that a large percentage of the text of the Prayer Book comes from the Bible. The 39 Articles make very clear that the Bible is the basis of the Prayer Book. The Prayer Book derives its whole authority from its grounding in the Word of God.

We have a wonderful Prayer Book for the exercise of godly worship to the glory of Christ Jesus, and we have Scriptures that have not changed and will not change. No new statements of theology need to be written. We don't need to receive a new word from God because it was all definitively written and graciously given to us by the saints 1,700 and some odd years ago. We need to follow our prayer to "read, mark, learn and inwardly digest the Word of God" *(The Book of Common Prayer,* Proper 28, pgs.184 and 236).

Studies show that, in Episcopal services, more Scripture is read than in any other denomination's services. All we have to do is become attentive to what's read, to understand it and live it.

The Apostle Paul reminded Timothy ...

"... how from infancy you have known the holy Scriptures, which are able to make you wise for salvation through faith in Christ Jesus. All Scripture is God-breathed and is useful for teaching, rebuking, correcting and training in righteousness, so that the man of God may be thoroughly equipped for every good work" (2 Timothy 3:15-17).

Scripture itself — and our own Church's witness to that Scripture — indicates the essential nature of the Bible for Christians. Why then do so few of our people know the Bible? In too many of our churches, the laity hear popular psychology, sociology, political theory and lots of gossip, but not the simple, enduring truth of God's Word.

When we try so hard to make our Church attractive and adapt new philosophical and cultural insights, we demonstrate a valid desire to be "relevant" — but if in becoming relevant we fail to ground our lives and teaching in Scripture, then we may gain popularity at the risk of our souls. If relevancy is to have integrity, it must conform to the Word of God. As a Church and as individuals, we must yield time to a diligent search of the Scriptures.

Our liturgy calls us to read Scripture — to "inwardly digest" the Word of God written — so that it might become the Word of God living in us. That is the ultimate goal of reading Scripture: that the Word of God might live in us, so that we become conformed to the Word of God written and are, in the process, *transformed* by it.

Living in us, the Word of God encourages us to be a bold witness for Christ Jesus. This is the next improvement we must make if we want to save our Church from itself. If you have never led anyone to faith in Jesus, it is time for you to do so. Develop a testimony and a knowledge of Scripture which allows you to lead a lost soul to the Lord with confidence. One of the troubles facing our Church is that we have turned eyes inward to focus on our new policies and changing theology, while our primary purpose — winning the world to Christ through missions and evangelism — has suffered. We can remedy that, beginning with our own witness.

Of course, you don't have to know the whole Bible

to be an effective witness.

Some years ago, I made a missions trip to Kenya. During that time, I went to visit with a missionary out in the bush, but when I arrived at the mission, he had already moved on. He left behind a native pastor who only knew three verses of Scripture. But he was preaching those three verses with utmost sincerity, and God was honoring it. I sat and spoke with this pastor in broken English. He was planning to study the Bible (as soon as he could get one) and continue winning his people to Christ. I gave him a New Testament that I knew he would read and study. I knew that, in the meantime, he would keep on telling people about Jesus with the three simple Scriptures he knew.

You and I can do at least as much. We may not be able to tell a person everything in the Bible, but we can impart the essence of the Gospel, and help them make a decision about it. If you love Christ, share Him with somebody! If Jesus Christ is the most important person in your life, then you know that He should be the most important person in the lives of your friends, acquaintances and family members. Tell them!

How can we say we love people, if we fail to share Jesus with them, knowing that their eternal lives pivot on their decision about Jesus?

How can we say we love our Church, if we don't boldly witness to Christ Jesus in it?

How can we say we love our priest and Church leadership, if we don't boldly witness to Christ Jesus before them?

Perhaps we don't witness to the power of Jesus before our fellow parishioners because we don't want to intimidate or frighten them. But the most important decision they can make is to accept Jesus Christ. You must love them enough to tell them the truth and risk their rejection.

We live under the false illusion that if we just love people enough and don't bother them, they will somehow see Jesus in us and be born again. It doesn't work that way. Silence is the enemy. The world is filled with good people who love others and don't intimidate them. But most of those people don't know the secret of salvation. Their lives are not a witness to Christ. Yours can be — if you open your mouth!

But opening your mouth isn't all of it. Your life, too, is an example of Christ in this world, and your body is the temple of His Holy Spirit. So, along with learning the Scriptures and presenting a bold verbal witness to Christ, we must also live holy lives.

Jesus said, "Be holy even as my Father who is in heaven is holy. That does not mean "holier than thou." That does not mean we who have a righteous theology are to walk around with a superior attitude toward our brethren who have been led astray or fallen away from the true faith. Holiness does not mean arrogance. It means being set apart for God's service. If you know that you are set apart for God, then holiness will flow naturally from that realization.

Yes, we all have habits and actions that we indulged before being set apart that we will want to give up when we begin leading a holy life. We will want to stop some behaviors because the presence of God in our lives will no longer permit them. And we will find ourselves doing other things we never dreamed we could do — because we have the strength of God inside.

As my grandmother once told me, "Remember, Todd,

that wherever you go in life, Jesus goes with you." I don't know about you, but I have been in some places where I would be ashamed to take Jesus. I have done some things that I am — and should be — ashamed of, and I have repented of them. Part of being holy — that is, "set apart" — is realizing that you are taking Jesus with you wherever you go, and that He is a witness to whatever actions you take.

This knowledge should give you a sense of discipline, a desire to go only to those places that will please God and to take only those actions that will please Him. Our Church needs that kind of discipline, but it will only find that discipline as you and I begin to be the holy people God called us to be, as we begin giving up old habits that we know are disgusting in God's sight and bring no glory to His kingdom; as we begin exhibiting the behaviors that are pleasing to God and bring glory to His name.

This all goes for me, too, of course. I don't live up to the standard of holiness I set for myself all of the time.

As a young man at my first clergy conference, I remember how disgusted I was at the after-hours talk of my fellow clergy. I heard the filthiest stories, the kind of language that would have embarrassed my father and his old friends (and *their* language embarrassed me). I realized, listening to them, that I was pointing a finger at those clergymen for their poor behavior, even while I still struggled with words I'd spoken thoughtlessly that I wouldn't want *anyone* to repeat. But day by day, I am striving to do better — and God has helped me to clean up my act.

If we wish to heal our Church — or even bring about a brand-new one — we need to take the time and energy required to exhibit the holiness and discipline God has called us to. You know, the best discipline you can exhibit for your own child is a love so great that the child wants to please you. I'd like to think that, after 50 years, I have begun to arrive at a place where I so much want to please God that I do what's right because I don't want to hurt Him.

That's the simplicity of holiness. You can learn that discipline, too.

All of us as Episcopalians are going to have to learn these disciplines if we really want to help birth a new, more faithful Church in the days ahead. We must learn and practice God's Word, develop a bold Christian witness and strive, with God's help, to walk in personal holiness. If every believer devoted himself to these tasks, we would see an incredible difference in every parish tomorrow.

Christianity is every Christian's work. As we each recognize this — and, recognizing it, step up to fulfill our part — the nature of the Church *will change.*

It will change because we have changed!

19 Early Christians, Early Church

"What do righteousness and wickedness have in common? Or what fellowship can light have with darkness?"

2 Corinthians 6:14

The Church was corrupt, filled with debauchery and despair.

The joy and fervor of early Christian faith had, over the centuries, given way to cynicism and infighting in the Church. Great preaching had devolved to convoluted theologies. The person in the pew understood neither the liturgy nor the meaning of Scripture. Grace was said to be mediated through the institutional Church and "forgiveness" was sold to pay both Church and secular debts.

Augustinian friar Martin Luther, preparing a series of lectures in the winter of 1512, undertook an intensive study of the Pauline epistles. As he studied Romans 1:16-17, a new light dawned in his mind and heart. In those moments, Luther discerned that salvation came through faith alone, *sola fide*, and not through works. When St. Paul's words came alive in Luther's understanding, he rediscovered the very heart of the biblical faith and witness. God had given him a place to stand from which to change both the Church and his world.

The Reformation was born.

As Luther made his rediscovery public, he joined the long line of inspired teachers and leaders (Joshua, the prophets, Nehemiah, John the Baptist, Paul, Augustine, Cranmer and Wesley among them) who, from the patriarchs onward, have preserved and renewed the Church.

Luther became the great *renovator* (not innovator) of the Church, striving to purify her from error and abuse. His 95 Theses against the abuse of indulgences — which he posted in the door of the Castle Church at Wittenberg on October 31, 1517 — provided the spark that ignited the Reformation. Luther then articulated the second great principle of the Reformation, *sola Scriptura* — "only by Scripture" can faith be proven and tested.

From this foundation, Luther is said to have uttered the words spoken during his trial in 1523: "Here I stand, I can do no other."

His stance sparked not only the Reformation but a long-term process of purification in the Church — the very idea, as the Reformers said, that the Church ought always to be in reformation. And so, through the centuries, God has used crises to challenge His Church, deepen our faith, heighten our commitment — and burn away the dross of apathy and despair.

Five hundred years after Luther, discontent and alienation again prevail — and the Church is once again in need of reformation and revival. And once again, the time has come not for innovation, but for renovation.

God is stirring the water, challenging Christians to take their stand.

Throughout the 1950's and into the mid 1960's, the Episcopal Church experienced an unprecedented period of growth. Our Church was reaching out to minorities and blue-collar families. New people were regularly joining our churches, swelling the confirmation classes. We were becoming an inclusive Church, moving away from a reputation as the Church of only the privileged or powerful.

But something happened. From 1965 to 1992, our Church shrank from 3.6 million members to 2.4 million — a loss of one-third of our membership. Those numbers are daunting enough, but translated they mean that nearly every Episcopalian can name family members and friends with whom they once attended Church, and now they no longer see. For many of us, those missing members are our own children, who've either dropped away from the Church altogether or sought spiritual nurturing elsewhere.

A once proud, growing and faithful Church — increasing to include a wide spectrum of Christians of differing skin color, social backgrounds and denominational experiences — has fallen from its once high calling into a morass of defeatism, apostasy and petty bickering.

A once certain Church, sure of its spiritual roots and of its faith and of its historic creeds, has now lost its theological moorings and wandered far afield in speculative thought and debate.

You've read in these pages many reasons for that unraveling. Now I want to share with you some ways to bring our Church to rebirth.

But first, let me make clear: not everything that has happened to the Episcopal Church in the past 30 years has been bad.

I am proud of our Church's willingness to take repeated stands for human dignity and human rights. I have been on the picket lines myself, and entered into protest marches on more than a few issues of civil rights. Although I had my doubts about the ordination of women, when I did my biblical and theological homework, I came to celebrate this expansion of the ordained ministry in the life of our Church.

But the debates that threaten the Church today go far beyond these issues. Bible teaching stands unequivocally against many of the teachings of our liberal leadership. No Christian, let alone an institution that calls itself Christian, can presume to bless what the Bible calls sin. The Episcopal Church cannot publicly affirm a sinful lifestyle and thereafter remain a healthy Christian Church. We will sicken at the heart, and eventually wither and die.

The Episcopal Church is also declining because we no longer live in a Christian culture, yet most of our churches have failed to adjust for that, to make the transition from local parish to missionary outpost. Faced with a nation of lost souls who either think they understand Christianity and have rejected it, or have never been exposed to the Gospel, the Episcopal Church must revamp its historic ways and return to its roots — the early Church.

The early Church was faced with the responsibility for taking a completely alien faith into a world that had never heard of it. The Jews were prepared to learn about the Messiah (although not all would accept Christ), but the idea of salvation through grace was foreign to all other cultures of the day. Every first-century

Christian was a missionary. As we move into the 21st century, we must realize that we, too, are that kind of missionary Church.

Today's circumstances are more accurately reflected in the first centuries of the Church's life than in the 15th through 20th centuries. So we now find ourselves applying the methods of the last 400 years to a world most of us no longer comprehend. To become a viable presence in this new environment, we must address several major issues in the next decade.

Church finance. For decades, we have funneled money out of parishes to support expanding bureaucracies at the diocesan and national levels. But the first-century Church needed no such organizations. Now that missionary and evangelism work must be shifted to the missionary outposts of local parishes, finances must also be shifted, with a lesser portion going to the diocese, and from dioceses in turn to the national office.

Church structure. Again, the national and diocesan offices must grow smaller — doing less, but also doing it better. Bishops must accept the leadership role played by their predecessors in the early Church: serving less as an administrator than as a pastor/teacher, discipling and training the laity in the work of evangelism and winning the lost to Christ.

Grass-roots education. Membership in the early Church involved a deeply personal commitment and a lengthy process of instruction in the fundamentals of the faith. Many Episcopalians today are biblically illiterate and doctrinally dysfunctional. If our members are each to function as missionaries in their own communities, we must get back to the basics, using the best methods of instruction and lifelong learning models available.

Evangelism and mission. For decades the local parish has been discouraged from the Gospel imperatives of evangelism and mission, which Episcopalians came to see as programs of the dioceses and the national Church. This was never the way in the first- and second-century Church, for the mission field was all around those new believers. Today the mission field again surrounds the Church — just down the street, just around the corner, just next door. We can no longer ignore the Lord's command to "go and make disciples." The Church that lives merely to maintain life within its own walls will soon die within those walls. We must embrace evangelism as the early Church did, and recommit to the biblical mission of all Christians, everywhere.

Church discipline. The Church of the early centuries was racially and culturally diverse. It was not, however, religiously diverse or doctrinally fuzzy. The Church understood itself as distinct from the emperor-worship of Rome and as spiritually unique from the other religions of its day. The Church established clear boundaries for believers, often through struggle and conflict, so that Christians knew where devotion to the world stopped and Christianity began. The Church must recover and reassert this unique calling and ministry, risking a deeper unpopularity in an increasingly idolatrous culture.

This return to the styles and substance of the early Church is occurring in many of our parishes today. Some of our churches are not reflecting the prevailing trends in the denomination toward cultural amalgamation and slow death — some are healthy, growing, leading lost souls into the kingdom and standing strong against the insidious campaign to give sin a comfortable place in our Church. What is the secret of these Churches?

20 Renewal

"I am making everything new!"

Revelation 21:5

Healthy, growing, Episcopal churches that are leading lost souls into the kingdom and standing strong to uphold the Scriptures and the Prayer Book are different from dying and declining churches because they have experienced renewal.

That fiery breath of the Holy Spirit has descended upon them and energized the congregations to change their community — and their world.

Do you know what the word "enthusiasm" means? It means to be filled with God, to be in God, to be excited about the things of God. I've seen this enthusiasm ignited in congregations when they receive the renewal that has been sweeping through local parishes for more than a decade now. Very few places in this world allow you to experience the joy and enthusiasm for God you find in renewed churches that are alive and vibrant.

But renewal has brought our Church more than enthusiasm. Let me mention just a few of the other ways God is moving in congregation after congregation to bring us back to our scriptural roots, and to bring life, salvation and hope into our Church once more.

- **Enhanced parochial ministry.** Renewal enhances the Episcopal Church's great ability to coalesce a parish, to care and to teach. We do parochial ministry reasonably well. Renewal refreshes an earlier vision of the parish as responsible for the "cure of souls."

- **Getting the "God talk" right.** Renewal also stirs in parishes the desire to learn our theology. Theology, at its root, means "God talk." Renewal helps us get our "God talk" right. Our theology must be consistent with the wisdom of the ages, in line with the thinking of the Church from ancient days. This does not mean that we ought not to use new words. It does not mean that we cannot bring fresh concepts to our theology. We must learn to speak of God and to do so both articulately and forthrightly.

  People and churches in renewal are searching the Scriptures diligently to find ways to talk about God's wonderful touch in our lives. Remember in the last chapter when I mentioned that God's people need to study and learn His Word? Renewal gives us the impetus to do so. Then as we begin to get our words straight, as we begin to get our talk right, we find ways to share with others the good things God has done in our lives.

- **Bible study and discipleship.** While we dare not devolve our Bible study and discipleship training into a kind of rigid fundamentalism or self-centered introspection, our lives must reflect scriptural truth. Renewal in the local Church can make discipleship and study a joy.

- **Clergy training in spiritual formation.** How many of us are willing, in our parishes, to give the extra dollars required to have a young man or woman live in our midst and receive training from a pastor we value and trust, whose leadership is fostering the development of a vibrant and renewed congregation? This is what happens in congregations experiencing renewal. Young clergy learn by doing hands-on ministry — gaining experience that can affect young lives forever.

By and large, Episcopal clergy receive their official training in seminaries largely divorced from the practice of ministry. Young and old people alike who hear God's call often leave the local scene where God is using them (and to which He has called them) for academic situations that strip them of the faith that has just begun to come to life in them! Often they return to parish ministry with the breath of the Spirit snuffed out by their training.

Churches in renewal are finding new ways to form and nurture clergy in their leadership of the Church, so that when they arrive at those less spiritually alive seminaries, they can release in those drab halls the spark of renewal — and then return from school ready for evangelism and excited about discipling new people and providing Spirit-inspired leadership.

Clergy in renewed churches don't come back from seminary looking at the laity simply as parishioners, but looking to them for support and strength as fellow travelers and workers together in the body of Christ.

• **Lay involvement.** Nowhere in the American and Canadian Church landscape have we seen more lay people get involved in the faith than through renewal. Without this renewal, the size of the Episcopal Church would be even smaller than it is now.

So far, however, we have failed to turn the corner from lay involvement to ministry. We must press forward for that day when every member becomes a minister. Remember I told you of Father Sam and "Pastor" Walker? Both were laymen when their inspired ministry affected my life incredibly. This is Jesus' model for ministry. When a minister models Christ for the congregation, the members themselves are inspired to minister, too.

• **Healing ministry.** The Episcopal Church has always believed in anointing and prayer for the sick. Yet so many of our Churches never experience the power of God released through a healing ministry! Prayer for the sick is not simply a ritual without meaning or substance. Rather, healing ministry is a living gift of the Spirit imparted by God.

Anyone who has ever cared for someone who is suffering cannot help but be interested in this ministry. I began to lay hands on the sick and pray with faith for their healing when I was swept up in renewal. And many of those I prayed with were miraculously healed!

One example. In 1987, I went to minister in Uganda with a couple of laypeople. At the Archbishop's palace in Kampala, one of my laymen left the table after dinner and went upstairs. On a large balcony of the house, he encountered a woman kneeling on all fours. He immediately offered help, and this rather large woman told him, "Several of my vertebrae are cracked and out of place."

This layman was a huge man, about six-foot-five, maybe 280 pounds. He picked the lady up, sat her in a chair, and said, "I'll go get Father Todd. We'll pray for you."

We prayed for her, and she was healed by the power of God! She got up and danced! That does wonders for your preaching, let me tell you!

Healing is one of the great gifts of renewal to the Church, but we cannot be naive, nor can we step beyond God's will in this matter. I remember a year when I had extended my hand in Jesus' name, and many had been healed. Then came the call, two o'clock in the morning, from some dear friends of our family. They told me Jeffrey, my godson, was being taken to the hospital even as we spoke. I rushed to his bedside and held him in my arms, praying for all I was worth that God would heal him.

God had seen fit to heal many total strangers for whom I had prayed without this much passion, but now I held Jeffrey in my arms as he died.

Within that year, two other young children died in my arms, while I prayed for them. I couldn't do anything except cry out to God. I still can't completely resolve these experiences in my own heart, because ultimately there is no humanly satisfying explanation of why God heals some and not others. Throughout that year, people tried to give me every sentimental or logical answer to why God didn't heal those children. But the truth of the matter is: God is God. He made the choice. I didn't. God is not mine to exercise. He is God. He is Father. But He isn't my buddy, and He does not operate at my beck and call.

Jerry Falwell was once asked to explain healing, since it seemed to happen quite a lot in his congregation. His answer: "I don't explain it. I just give thanks for it." Healing touches the deepest mystery of our lives. Like Pastor Falwell, I give thanks for it — but I never let myself believe I can control it.

- **We do conferences.** One characteristic of people in renewal is that they want to know more about renewal, and they are willing to travel miles to learn what they want to know. Sometimes, these conferences are little more than pep rallies, and that is important because heaven knows sometimes we just need cheering up. God honors it when we come together, and we have much to celebrate as God touches our lives.

But more than pep rallies, we need conferences that train and equip us to be the kind of

Christians God is calling us to be. The ministry I am affiliated with, Episcopalians United, produces some of these conferences. A lot of times, I have the heaviest briefcase, and I have come the most miles to speak at the conference, but that doesn't make me an expert. We are all in this together, and I am struggling just like you are. I have weak points and doubts. I have cried a bucket of tears. However, I cannot give in — and you cannot give in — to the tendency in Christianity to point a finger at the next person and say, "He really has it all together. I am a very poor example, but he gives a good witness." You see, the next lost soul I encounter won't have someone else to look to for an example. He'll only have me to model Christ for him.

God wants it that way. You may well be the only example of Christianity many people ever see. That's why you need to be the very best you can be in Christ Jesus. That's why I personally need to be the very best I can be. That's why we need to encourage each other. We need to grow as we come together, pushing, helping, encouraging, strengthening each other forward in Christ Jesus. Paul said, "I press toward ... the upward call of God in Christ Jesus" (Philippians 3:14, NKJV). This should be the intent and the purpose of our conferences and seminars — pressing on for the upward call.

- **Evangelism.** We've argued about evangelism for 25 years in the Episcopal Church, and we've done very little of it. We have failed to put the priority of the Great Commission in its proper place. We were called into being by Christ Jesus for a purpose. We have not paid much attention to that purpose, and I believe the Lord is now permitting us to be in an environment where we will not survive if we do not do what He has asked and even commanded us to do. This is why He has blessed us with an enhanced vision and desire for evangelism through renewal.

People in renewal lead other people to Christ because they genuinely love Christ and genuinely share His love for the lost. More of us need to awaken to evangelism — not only to keep our churches alive, but to keep our own souls alive. If you want to keep your faith fresh and vital, give it away! Faith is one thing you have more of as you give more away. When you stop giving it away, it begins to wither and die.

And people come to Christ one person at a time. There's no corporate salvation. Kathryn Kuhlman used to say, "God has no grandchildren." Your parents faith doesn't make you a Christian. If that's true, then many of the setbacks and failures we see represented in the Church today will pass. Only those who are leading people into a living relationship with Jesus Christ today will see their faith survive tomorrow.

I may not win everyone to Christ. I may not even win very many. But between now and the time I die, I am going to lead at least some into the Kingdom. I don't think when I reach the Judgment Seat that God will look at my clerical collar and automatically let me in. But I trust that when I meet Jesus face to face, I will honestly be able to look Him in the eye and say, "Most of the time when I had the opportunity to share You with someone — I did that. I didn't always do the best job, but I sure tried my best."

People in renewal are inspired to win others to Christ. Maybe you don't invite anyone to Church because you feel too embarrassed by some of the things that our leaders do from time to time. Imagine how embarrassed God must be! You can stand a little more embarrassment. Whatever our leaders say and do, God's Word is true and He will honor it.

You didn't sign on with Christ to have the best of every situation. Paul said we signed on as slaves of Christ. Slaves have no right to refuse an order. Jesus told you, "Go into all the world and preach the good news to all creation" (Mark 16:15). Jesus said to you, "Blessed are you when people insult you, persecute you and falsely say all kinds of evil against you because of me" (Matthew 5:11). Persecution isn't comfortable, but it is a path of blessing open to you as you witness to salvation through Christ.

Renewal gives individual Christians and local bodies all the same strengths that powered the early Church. In renewal, our churches display that same dynamic life, the life the Church spread across the known world through the salvation message. We can do the same! Our own Church leadership may be standing against this vision right now, but there is no cause for despair when God has so richly blessed us with renewal and all its strengths.

"Let us fix our eyes on Jesus, the author and perfecter of our faith ..."

21 Episcopalians United

"... Christ in you, the hope of glory."

Colossians 1:27

Two stories from the Bible speak powerfully to those of us despairing over events in the Episcopal Church.

First, in Luke 5:1-11, we find a group of fishermen, out in their boats on the Sea of Galilee all night, catching nothing. I have tried to eat fish from the Sea of Galilee on several occasions, and it is not to my liking, but for some reason the Romans liked this fish; it could be dried and stored and transported well. So any fishermen licensed by the Roman government who could catch those fish could make a great deal of money in Jesus' day. But this particular day, they had fished all night and caught nothing — probably not an experience they had very often. No doubt they were tired, frustrated, angry, despairing.

In their anger and despair, they sailed into shore, ready to give up, and they did something sort of unusual. They stopped to listen to someone who was speaking in the natural amphitheater between the Capernaum hillside and the Sea of Galilee. Usually when

I come in at the end of a hard day — especially if I've accomplished nothing and feel angry and frustrated — I don't feel like stopping to hear any new street preacher. But these fellows did. They were despairing, yet they were willing to listen. I suspect that Jesus had seen them out at sea. He knew they had caught nothing. He could see in their faces and the tired slumping of their bodies that they were frustrated, despairing. And I think because they stopped to listen to Him, the heart of Jesus was moved, and He challenged them to go back out to sea, casting their nets on the other side of the boat.

What would you do? They had been fishing all night in that same sea. Going back out to sea must have seemed an impossible task to these tired, despairing men. Yet when Jesus gave them this word, they did it. They put back out to sea and caught so many fish their nets couldn't contain them! They were despairing, yet they were willing to listen.

After our long night of struggle in the Episcopal Church, some of us feel a deep sense of despair. Are we also willing to listen?

Now shift back from New Testament to Old Testament times. In First Samuel 17, we find the familiar story of David and Goliath.

King Saul and his army were besieged by the Philistines. Wasn't he always besieged by the Philistines? It seems that, no matter what Saul did, he had the Philistines mad at him. In this case, as in most of the battles of the Israelites we read about, the odds were stacked against the good guys. Four thousand to 6,000 Israelites against more than 35,000 Philistines. Even if I knew I was with God's people, I believe I would find those odds intimidating.

Furthermore, every morning, the Israelites had to face thousands of Philistine warriors who sent out their mightiest champion, a giant named Goliath, to taunt them. I am 5 feet, 11 inches tall, but next to an eight-foot-tall man, I believe I would feel even smaller. I know when I first saw Wilt Chamberlain, I felt about three feet tall. So Goliath was quite awe-inspiring as he called out his taunts, demanding that an Israelite come out and fight him. Of course, the Israelites cowered before him, and the situation seemed bleak.

Then into the camp came David, a young boy whose only life experience had been minding his father's sheep. He brought some supplies to his older brothers. And he heard the taunts of the giant Goliath. But David remembered what everyone else had forgotten. He remembered that the Israelites — not the Philistines — were God's chosen people. To everyone's amazement, David marched out onto the field to fight the giant.

The rest of the army, cowering back behind the Israelite lines, was thinking, "Goliath is so big, I'll never beat him." But David, marching out to battle in the power of God, was thinking: "He's so big, I can't miss."

And of course, he didn't.

What made the difference? Goliath was the same giant. The armies were still terribly mismatched. The situation had not changed — only the spirit inside one boy.

We in the Episcopal Church face problems today that seem huge, even overwhelming. Yet the truth is, the problems are so big that, with God's help, we can't miss them! Like those disciples, we may be despairing after our long night of struggle — but if we're willing to listen and obey, a great reward in the form of ministry awaits us!

We need to take the presence of Christ Jesus in ourselves more seriously. "Christ in you" is not a platitude. Why are we dismayed in the face of a Church leadership we do not understand and that appears to be guiding the Church into apostasy? We shouldn't be dismayed, for we have Christ in us! The Bible tells us "greater is He that is in you, than he that is in the world" (1 John 4:4, KJV). Jesus Himself tells us the gates of hell shall not prevail against His Church (Matthew 16:18).

Jesus will prevail. His Church will prevail. Everything else is just passing away. Our current leadership will die one day, as will you and I. It is not for us to condemn others, but to witness to them of He who is in our lives. Even now the enemy is at work, but Jesus will prevail. I know a God whose mercy knows no limits and whose power has no restraints.

This is the great strength of renewal: Jesus alive in you and me. As this glorious message of renewal reaches more and more churches, it is our hope that the membership of the Church will be awakened, that the dormant faith now incipient in the Church will become more obvious, that we will begin to be a people who are enthusiastic for the ministry and witness of Jesus Christ.

For this cause, the ministry of Episcopalians United began — and today fights hard to organize both laity and numerous clergy to stand up and be counted for the sake of truth and the future of our Church. Our work in ministry during the past several years has taught us five key values:

Ministry: We believe lay Episcopalians are the primary ministers of the Gospel.

Mission: We believe the primary mission of the Church is to nurture people in the knowledge and love of Jesus as both Lord and Savior.

Unity: We are committed to unity in the Church through confession of a common faith in Jesus Christ as Lord.

Methods: We seek to be active, not reactive, in asserting the essentials of the Christian faith and building up the Church in every good work.

Prayer: We believe constructive change results only from action rooted in prayer.

While we have focused on these values, we have gained a profound respect for the work, faith and ministry of the laity. We believe our Church will change constructively only when the Lord's voice is truly reflected and heeded in the voices of her general membership.

The focus of our work is on the revelation of God, the renewal of His people and the reformation of His Church. We work aggressively to awaken an increasing number of Episcopalians out of their apathy to face the crisis in our Church. In the midst of the fight, we have neither lost our hope for the Church nor lost our confidence that God has a much brighter future in store for the Episcopal Church. We believe the incredible growth of the Church during the 1950's and 1960's was only a prelude to the Church we can be if:

- we repent of our faithless floundering and return to the Lord. We must encourage and expect men and women to repent of sin and return to the Lord, for this is the will of God who loves and cares for us.
- we seek to provide clear, consistent moral teachings of the Scriptures rather than caving

in to the anchorless and desperate assertions of our secular society and some of our own leaders.

- we teach and preach the Bible as the Word of God written — not as a hammer by which to beat people into submission, but as a clear and divine guide to healthy and holy living.
- we present Jesus Christ as the Son of God who was "crucified, dead and buried" for our sins and whom God raised from the dead to be Savior and Lord for all humanity.
- we become a people of prayer, and our Churches once again become houses of prayer.

How can we accomplish this — and what is Episcopalians United doing to make this vision a reality?

Ours is the part of the activist. You will recall that earlier we defined the liberal/revisionists of our Church as the more "activist" of the factions. We are reclaiming that ground for the conservative/orthodox viewpoint, because conservative inaction is allowing liberals to move the Church further and further from God's Word and His calling.

Conservatives and moderates have worked hard at being fair and gracious, giving a breadth of interpretation to many Church doctrines. Liberals and revisionists are clear, precise and resolute about their intentions. Their position neither waivers nor varies. They appear willing to breach the unity of the Church irreparably to get what they want today. Faced with such opposition, the even-handedness and stolid silence of the more orthodox has been interpreted as weakness, and our liberal brethren have attacked at the point of this apparent weak link.

We can no longer afford to remain passive.

The work of Episcopalians United, then, is to *actively* organize, persuade, challenge and equip faithful Episcopalians to make a difference.

- We constantly seek to address critical issues where the battle is hottest.
- We are activists on the frontlines of Church conventions.
- We offer both laity and clergy solid, alternative resources to the watered-down tools provided by the morally compromised national leadership.
- We organize media campaigns, letter-writing and petition drives, and appropriate demonstrations.
- We have been and are in the trenches with men and women who depend on us for research, analysis, advice and encouragement.

We believe Christians like you are called not to passive belief, but to struggle in the spiritual arena for the souls of a fallen, yet loved, humanity. Episcopalians United has a membership of some 25,000 throughout the United States who have taken up the call to righteous action and belief in the Church. They are people like you and me, traditional Episcopalians who want to see our Church returned to her biblical footing. With their financial support, volunteer help and prayers, our organization has become a leading voice for conservatives in our Church.

By now I trust that you, too, have come to realize that the traditional path of studying and living God's Word is the best (and only Christian) path available to the Episcopal Church. I invite you to join me and other

Christians in Episcopalians United.

Among the most important outreaches of our ministry are:

Biblically sound tracts, videos, books and literature. Because the national leadership is today in the hands of liberals and revisionists, much of the literature provided on the national level is tainted with "incarnational theology," inclusivity, and other non-biblical ideas and themes. Where are conservative and traditional parishes to look for biblically sound doctrinal materials for adult education? How can we learn, study and inwardly digest the Scriptures without proper tools for study? Episcopalians United is joyful in its status as one of the largest producers of biblically sound tracts, videos and books to supplement adult Christian education in our Church.

Intercessory prayer. Liberal and revisionist dogmas of social improvement, civil rights, and enhanced justice for all are important goals — but the primary goal of the Christian Church is to win the world to Christ. This will never happen without the constant prayer of God's people. With the winds of renewal blowing through our congregations has come the desire for better, more effective prayer within our parishes. Episcopalians United has led the way with a monthly program of prayer and Bible study, the Joshua Circle. This ministry has become one of the largest intercessory prayer ministries in the life of our Church.

Seminars and conferences. When the Church structure itself became compromised by liberal/revisionist theologies and ideas, concerned Episcopalians had to look outside the national leadership for direction in reviving and rebirthing our Church. God has blessed

Episcopalians United with a gift for informing and mobilizing conservative/traditional Episcopalians to work and pray their way toward a more faithful Church. Our conferences and seminars have changed lives and helped parishes across the nation.

Grassroots outreach. At the last General Convention, when "local option" became the catchword (more on that later), grassroots efforts became even more important. We are a national network of theologically conservative Episcopalians working in unity at the parish and diocesan levels to change the future for our Church. In this way, we can do more in the next few years toward constructive change in the life of the Church than perhaps any amount of campaigning at General Conventions and among the House of Bishops.

Remember that I mentioned evangelism is only really accomplished one soul at a time, person to person? We have reached the stage in our history where it is possible to change the entire Church, one parish at a time, diocese by diocese. I'll explain why that's true in the next chapters. For now, I encourage you to play a more active role in the reform and renewal of our Church.

22 Local Option: God's Secret Weapon?

"And as for you, brothers, never tire of doing what is right."

2 Thessalonians 3:13

In an old joke, a hellish boss posts a sign that says, "The beatings will continue until morale improves." In the Episcopal Church, it seems irregular ordinations and flouting of Church doctrine will continue until orthodox laity and clergy surrender — or stop this vicious process.

This has never been more obvious than today, when the national Church's direction calls for "local option." What is it?

Local option is the continuing ruling of the 1991 and 1994 General Conventions allowing bishops, local parishes and dioceses to make their own judgments on difficult issues rather than relying on the Scriptures or consensus.

The fact of local option (whether it has been codified or not) occurs when bishops act on their own belief, in morals or theology or both, without paramount regard for the consensus of other bishops. The national Church then recedes into the background. This is already happening in our Church, for better or worse.

For instance, in the matter of ordaining noncelibate homosexuals (or noncelibate single people of any persuasion), local option allows for bishops to "continue in trust and *koinonia*, ordaining only persons we believe to be a wholesome example to their people, according to the standards and norms set forth by the Church's teaching." This ruling (Guideline 8b from the *Continuing the Dialogue* document) is so imprecise that bishops can ordain noncelibate homosexuals in good conscience and cite Guideline 8b as their justification — following the dictates of whatever they believe to be wholesome rather than what the Bible makes clear is acceptable. The House of Bishops rejected the sane alternative — placing a moratorium on ordination of noncelibate homosexuals until the dialogue process could be completed — in favor of this weak stance, abandoning the authority of the national Church leadership to that of the local leadership.

As long as the national leadership thus passes the buck of its indecision down to the local church, no real legislation can be passed at a national level, and certainly no "mind of the Church" resolutions can be taken seriously, for the national Church has lost touch with its mind — that is "the mind of Christ."

What has to change? Liberal and revisionist people and organizations must stop looking to the General Convention to legitimize their causes and concerns, and conservatives cannot expect the General Convention to "fix" the Church for us.

So, will local option work for us or against us? The answer can be found in Joshua 5:13-14, where Joshua faced a similar unknown:

Now when Joshua was near Jericho, he looked

up and saw a man standing in front of him with a drawn sword in his hand. Joshua went up to him and asked, "Are you for us or for our enemies?"

"Neither," he replied, "but as commander of the army of the Lord I have now come." Then Joshua fell face down to the ground in reverence.

The angel told Joshua he was not there to take sides, but to take *over*. I believe God is arranging a supernatural takeover of the Episcopal Church, in the guise of local option. We may wonder whether local option works *for* us or *against* us, but the answer lies *in* us. If we have chosen the Lord's side, rather than asking Him to take ours, and fall down in reverence before Him, then we will triumph.

Although in the name of local option the Church most likely will allow each diocese to ordain the priests of its own choosing and to bless same-sex unions, local option is not all bad news. The good news is that, beginning at the parish level, God could use this fractured Church to raise up a more faithful and biblical version of His ideal. This is, after all, where our Church has her roots: it was not until the end of the 19th century that the vision of a national entity with a Catholic ethos arose in our nation. Before then, the Episcopal Church was a largely congregationalist federation of dioceses.

Beneath the clamor of sword-rattling division over issues, recent Conventions have witnessed (and fostered) the death of one dream — a national Church — and the re-emergence of an older reality: a gathering of parishes around a single bishop loosely related to other bishops. A reformed Church will need three essential ingredients:

- Bishops who serve the local congregation through a teaching office that embodies the Christian faith.
- Clergy who equip the laity for ministry rather than limiting it to themselves.
- An informed and more deeply committed laity, ready to take its rightful place in the ministry and governance of the Church.

The tide for Church reform is growing and has been enhanced by the advent of local option. We are increasingly a congregational Church — and only those structures that truly assist the local congregation and its perceived mission will thrive.

The times ahead may be difficult as conservatives, moderates, liberals, revisionists and just plain folks move into the reality of a reinvented Episcopal Church, but much good can yet come of local option:

- Loyalty will no longer flow upstream — which is critical since the national leadership is so far upstream from the folks in the pews that, by and large, it does not deserve their loyalty.
- We will refocus our energies to nurture local congregations.
- Although some will decry the loss of a strong national program, a new and powerful dynamic, consistent with our heritage, will reemerge.
- We will rediscover the local parish as the primary reality of the Church.
- Parishes will be the places where evangelism happens and from which the mission of the Church proceeds.
- The role of bishop will take on deeper spiritual and teaching dimensions.

The national organization, if it still exists, will perforce grow leaner and less powerful as parishes and dioceses exercise their local option to withhold funding from a structure that no longer represents or aids them. Local option then takes on the task of downsizing, forcing cuts of all national structures that require a large staff.

The bureaucracy will and should be diminished. In order to sustain themselves and aid the Church, national and diocesan leadership must concentrate on empowering the local church instead of "nationalizing" ministry. Ideally, under local option, the purpose of our General Convention would be to network, share our common practices of worship, and study Scripture, faith, social issues and evangelism.

The death or radical transformation of the national organization does not signal the death of the Episcopal Church in any way. An antiquated bureaucracy is dying, but our focus need not turn inward to death. Rather, we can now focus on rebuilding the Church to meet the needs of an increasingly diverse population in the United States and around the world. The downsizing of our national offices is not a cause for alarm, especially because the past few years make obvious the incredible gap between the national leadership and the membership of the Episcopal Church.

At the last General Convention, for instance, liberal/revisionist thinkers "owned" the presidency of both legislative houses. Through these positions, they control membership and leadership on all major committees. They control the Church press and conduct carefully managed press conferences with the secular media by selecting mostly like-minded bishops as spokespersons.

Liberals and revisionists have consolidated political power at the national level. The system has thus been staffed and managed to frustrate and minimize conservative forces and intentions for years.

It can't last. Over the long run, a government that must coerce its citizens cannot sustain itself. The government of the Episcopal Church, grossly out of touch with the men and women who occupy the pews, is feeling the effects of local option in this way: the laity is becoming reluctant to pay the bills for nonrepresentational leadership.

A lesson from secular politics deserves a hearing: liberals shout and march, but conservatives send money. In the final analysis, the vote that counts is written on checks in the plate, and the ballot box is passed every Sunday. Blunt talk about the Church we love? Perhaps, but men and women have grown tired of supporting a Church bureaucracy that is not only failing to advance the Gospel but that appears increasingly opposed to it.

The stewardship vote is destined to be "no" to national leadership and "yes" to local congregations. Local option, if allowed to take its true course, will finally level the playing field among Episcopal churches. Gay churches, straight churches, New Age churches, and orthodox churches will all have to compete freely and financially to speak to a culture sliding into a swamp.

Here, the traditionalists and the churches in renewal have the edge — because we know that God is faithful, and His Word does not return empty. He will bless what He will bless. He will continue to raise up churches and ministries that speak His Word. The church that triumphs will be the one that has placed itself not on the liberal side or the conservative side, but on God's side.

Thus all the blessings of local option will grow and blossom in local churches and dioceses where clergy and laity believe in the Church's scriptural foundation and are willing to take on the role of missionary that the first century Christians fulfilled.

You ask: what if I don't live in a faithful parish? Or, what if my priest is not willing to stand up against liberal and revisionist pressures? What can I do?

If your local parish is not faithful to God's Word and is resistant to renewal, I don't want to discourage you, for there is much you can do to strengthen your own Christian walk and help your church. However, I must tell you that you are a forerunner of Christians of the next generation who will live in an environment even more hostile to God's Word. Take heart, for your example and your testimony can be a guiding light to the Christians who will come in succeeding generations.

As a Christian in an apostate church, you must work harder at your faith and design new ways to survive and thrive without the support of your church.

The first and most important direct action you must take is to meet the Christian education needs of your children or grandchildren if your church is not doing so. God calls you to provide for and manage your own family before you take on a leadership role in the church. And naturally, you should be most concerned about your own family before you worry about yourself and the condition of your congregation.

Even if you were in a church where the Christian education system was adequate, it would still be incumbent upon you to teach the Gospel to your children at home. Home is the first place where youngsters should see the Gospel modeled, and family Bible study should be the first place they learn of the wondrous love of Jesus. Do not imagine that Sunday School takes the place of a family altar — even if it is a very good Sunday School. Do not neglect the Christian education of your children.

Next, find fellow believers in your own area. How do you find them? Where are they? I can help you there, for Episcopalians United has numerous local chapters. Our members believe in the words of Scripture and the Prayer Book, and many are members of thriving churches in renewal. Although your parish may not have its own chapter, your diocese may. Through Episcopalians United, you can connect with others who hold your beliefs and enlist aid in locating believers within your own parish and diocese. It is not always easy to stand up alone, but Ecclesiastes 4:12 (KJV) says, "And if one prevail against him, two shall withstand him; and a three-fold cord is not quickly broken." Even two or three believers united can stand together in Christ's name and make a difference.

Now, you and two or three other Christians may feel alone and outnumbered in a parish that doesn't believe the same Gospel you do. Learn to build each other up. Intercessory prayer and Bible study are two keys to growing in Christ, and to growing closer together. And don't keep these sessions to yourself — you may be surprised that many of the people in your church who can't be identified as believers really are seeking more substantive guidance. The invitation to join real believers in fellowship, prayer and study may be just what they need to open their hearts to the Word of God and the message of salvation. Once again, I would offer you the services of Episcopalians United's "Joshua Circle." This is the largest intercessory prayer group in the Episcopal Church, and we can provide you with resources for Bible study, effective prayer and spiritual growth.

You and the few believers in your area can actually shape your parish as laity. You don't need (although it would be nice to have!) a priest who shares your belief. Episcopal trends are moving us toward a Church where the action happens at the local level. The trend within a trend is that the action will be generated among the laity — not necessarily the clergy. You and the believers of your parish must regularly gather together to build each other up, and invite non-believing Episcopalians to join you. I guarantee you will find no more motivating and bonding experience than the first time your small group leads another soul to Christ.

You and whatever believers you find within your church can grow in Christ as you stick together, stand strong, and build each other up. It is my prayer for you, and my belief, that God will honor your faithfulness with the blessing of the Holy Spirit. Then you may find that the real ministry of your church isn't flowing from Sunday morning services or pastoral counseling sessions, but through you and the Christians who have joined together to honor God and glorify Christ through prayer and study together.

It would not surprise me if that move of God among you eventually changes the face of your church... not immediately, and perhaps not without struggle, but as you and the believers of your church are focused on God and trusting His ways, He will bless your company.

You are also responsible for working together with the clergy of your parish constructively and in a spirit of love and compassion. Remember, if your parish is truly

186 • Steadfast Faith

apostate, your priest may not even share your faith in Christ. Try to determine whether your priest believes in the Gospel of redemption and forgiveness of sins through the sacrifice of Christ. I think you will probably find that your priest is simply a timid believer who is being swept along by the liberal/revisionist thinking of our times.

If you are united in faith with your priest, you can be a positive and emboldening influence on him or her. Even if your priest denies the saving power of Christ, you can still maintain your standards of love and compassion as you confront unsound doctrine and encourage a more scripturally based theology and an awareness and respect for the doctrines of the Church, the Scriptures and Prayer Book.

These courses of action will help you and the other Christians of your parish to survive — even thrive — in your spiritual walk, in spite of the prevailing liberal spirit in an apostate parish. Some other practical steps you can take toward the redemption of your parish:

1. You and other believers should attend the annual meeting of your parish. Pay special attention when electing leadership and delegates to your diocesan convention, and don't be afraid to ask the candidates about their views and theology before voting. Whenever you can responsibly do so, you may want to consider running for office, and definitely volunteer to serve your parish in its many ministries.

2. Ask your rector to keep the parish informed openly about issues facing the Church, including key issues such as homosexuality and

inclusivity, which strike at the heart of our faith. Let the rector know that you support forums and discussion within the parish on these issues. The newspaper of Episcopalians United, *United Voice*, can also keep you informed, and we invite you to make copies for your friends and fellow parishioners.

3. Show your support for the Frey Canon and work to have your vestry and annual meeting adopt it as parish policy. The Frey Canon simply states that ordained Episcopal clergy will refrain from sexual practices outside of Holy Matrimony. Encourage your vestry and your delegates to diocesan convention to adopt this biblical standard as parish and diocesan policy.

4. In parish newsletters, diocesan newspapers and local papers, publish articles and letters that promote reliance on Scripture and the Prayer Book and the biblical standard in issues of human sexuality. You are free to submit my articles from *United Voice* under my byline if you find they fit with the issues under discussion in your parish.

5. Join Episcopalians United to network with other Episcopal believers. We also have a thorough resource center, including tracts, surveys, studies and videotapes which can help you and the other believers of your parish. Supplying us with a parish list, or the names of other believers in your parish, would help us build our base of traditional/orthodox believers working to bring reform and renewal

to our Church.

6. If your area does not have a local Episcopalians United chapter, work with others to establish one by joining forces with believers in other parishes. We can provide you with information about supporting churches, chapters and individuals in your area. We also give you and other believers the opportunity to address issues on a national level when necessary through petitions and other communiqués to leadership that pack a fair punch when they carry the signatures of thousands of believers like you.

7. Work with others to organize conferences on important issues. Episcopalians United can help in developing conferences and seminars.

8. Write to your bishop, clergy and deputies to express your concerns. They need to hear from you.

9. Find out what percentage of parish funds is sent to the national Church office through the diocese, and prayerfully consider withholding that percentage from your own giving as an expression of disapproval for the current chaotic situation engendered by national leadership. If God leads you to make this move as a matter of conscience, you could keep the withheld funds in an escrow account with the intention of giving them when the national leadership has come back to biblical foundations. You can notify your parish of this action and your intent to give these funds later.

10. Speak up. If you remain in your parish but do not voice your concerns, it is difficult to see any benefit to the Church. With the *love of Christ*, speak your mind and confront when necessary.

If you are one of few believers in an apostate church, you may feel like you're swimming upstream — but you *can* make a difference. Conservatives and traditionalists, united, are now beginning to have a positive and lasting impact on our Church.

Now is not the time to give in to despair and the temptation to depart in silence for greener pastures. Rather, now is the time to stand and be counted. Working together, we can and will bring our Church to a greater faithfulness and a clearer witness. The road ahead will not be easy, but we are progressing. Now is the time to become more active at the local level, where all lasting change in our Church must begin.

There is hope — and you are one reason for it.

23 Why I Still Have Hope

"I will give you thanks, for you answered me; you have become my salvation. The stone the builders rejected has become the capstone; the Lord has done this, and it is marvelous in our eyes."

Psalm 118:21-23

In the amusing and uncannily historically accurate Broadway musical 1776, the nervous sponsors and author of the *Declaration of Independence* are reassuring each other of the document's merit while it is under debate in the Continental Congress. They compare this maddening wait for approval to the birth process — in fact, the birth (or hatching) of an eagle.

Benjamin Franklin and John Adams congratulate Thomas Jefferson with these words about the new nation about to be "hatched":

And just as Tom here has written,
Though the shell may belong to Great Britain,
The eagle inside belongs to us!

The shell of the Episcopal Church is being fragmented from within. But this fragmenting turns out to be a good and hopeful development, for it is caused by an emerging Episcopal Church pecking its way out — and the eagle inside belongs to us.

The current fragmentation of our Church offers hope, because it has forced Episcopalians of all types to realize they can no longer cloak themselves in church-on-Sunday and hope that enough of it wears off on them to sustain them until next week. My heart grieves that the Episcopal Church has become a place for people who think of themselves as Christians by birth, who believe salvation came with their citizenship, and who see no need for a personal commitment to Christ Jesus.

We built churches to cater to people who wanted to be ministered to, and then we brought those people in. We tried to bring the whole world into the Church and to be its chaplain, but we forgot how to disciple people to propagate the kingdom of God. As long as the children of most Episcopalian families were born right into the Church and stayed here, we didn't feel we had to go out into the highways and hedges to compel others to come in.

The darkness in our culture and the fragmenting of our Church have finally brought us to a point where we recognize that chaplaincy's day is over, and the day of individual responsibility — of each Christian as missionary — has begun. History instructs that culture, once it's headed down a dark path, continues further into darkness — sometimes for hundreds of years — before a new light dawns. In these dark times, each bearer of God's light must know how to nurture and share it. This is the great hope for our Church, and it begins with each individual Episcopalian.

So — how can I be assured that I am part of the renewal and revival of the Episcopal Church?

On a personal level, my role begins with repentance. We may think we have nothing to repent of, but sometimes pride blinds us. The next time someone asks who you are, and Jesus' name doesn't come up in your answer, you may need to repent — from the kind of pride that makes you think you would be anything without Jesus.

We bring nothing to Him, but He freely gives us everything. Your successful marriage and family shouldn't be a point of pride to you. You should fall on your knees and thank God for them. Your good job and bank account, your musical talents and nice looks, your stock-market savvy and innate business sense — all these are gifts from God. Whenever you pat yourself on the back for the great deal you just closed or the smashing appearance you just made — that's when you need to repent.

I know this because I am an expert on pride. I have been dealing with it in my own life for years. I have found that repentance doesn't begin when we're feeling good about ourselves and proud of our accomplishments. It begins when we are convicted of our utter emptiness without God.

I was speaking at a conference in Ridgecrest, North Carolina, talking about the fact that much of our trouble in the Episcopal Church stems from two irreconcilable views: either man is fallen and nothing without God, or man is basically good and needs only to dispel ignorance to achieve his full potential. A dear lady, an older Episcopalian woman, came up to me after my lecture and said, "I am so angry with you, I can't stand it. I believe that man is basically good, and the root of our problems is ignorance. We just need to be more loving sometimes — that's what it means to be a Christian. But you just told me that's not true. You just told me I'm not a Christian. You were supposed to make me feel better than that."

Unilaterally, Episcopalians need to repent of that attitude. Our Church has fostered an image that the mission of the Church is to make you feel good, and we have tried to fulfill that mission by bringing in a lot of inclusive and incarnational theology that concentrates on everyone feeling good but doesn't win any souls to the Kingdom of God. In fact, this attitude endangers the salvation of lost souls by telling them they can continue in their sin as long as they feel good about it.

News flash: it is not the Church's responsibility to make you feel good. Rather, the Church is called to speak the words that bring souls to conviction and show them the way to repentance and salvation.

The first step we can make personally is repentance. Then if we want to be part of the renewal and revival of our Church, we must become mature in our faith. Are you growing daily in Christ? Let me share with you my description of the complete, mature Christian. The mature Christian has entered into a personal relationship with Christ Jesus by:

- Inviting the Lord into his/her life (Revelation 3:20, John 14:23, John 17:3).
- Learning to listen to the Lord through regular Bible study and prayer (Philippians 4:6, 2 Timothy 3:16-17).
- Putting into practice those things that indicate "new life" in Christ (Philippians 2:1-18, Colossians 3, 2 Timothy 2:15-16).
- Practicing Christian humility and living in the fullness of God's love (1 Peter 5:5, Acts 20:18-19).

- Exercising Christian virtues of mercy and persistence (James 3:13-18, Romans 5:1-5, Hebrews
  12:1-11).

The mature Christian has also entered into a personal relationship with the Lord's family, the Church, by:

- Finding good fellowship and becoming a
  responsible, contributing and positive partici-
  pant (1 Corinthians 12:12-13:13).
- Publicly proclaiming a personal commitment to
  Christ and new life in Him (1 Timothy 3:6-12).
- Learning of the family heritage — the customs,
  traditions and teaching of the Church (2
  Timothy 3:14-15).
- Regularly attending worship and entering into
  determined periods of study with others for
  further growth and maturity in the faith (Acts
  2:41-42).

The mature Christian has accepted responsibility for
fulfilling Christ's Great Commission (Matthew 28:19-20)
by:

- Asking for and receiving the baptism in the
  Spirit, thereby receiving "power" for witness
  and ministry (Acts 2:38-39, John 3:5, John
  14:12-26).
- Actively seeking to share faith in Christ with
  those who do not yet know Him (Matthew
  28:19-20).
- Continuing to grow in Christ through giving
  and receiving ministry (Galatians 5:16-6:10, 1
  Corinthians 12:1-11, 28-31, Ephesians 4:2-16).

These steps toward maturity will launch your personal part in the renewal of the Episcopal Church. But, as
the last description of maturity indicates: the acid test of

renewal has nothing to do with how many people raise their hands in worship or receive the gift of tongues. Rather, the acid test of renewal is whether the Church is seeing souls won into the Kingdom of God. Yet I've come to believe that for many Episcopalians, the word "evangelism" is fear-provoking.

A number of years ago, a survey was taken before a national convention, and the results indicated laity felt "evangelism" was the top priority of the Church. We created a national office for evangelism. We held conferences. Talk about the subject multiplied exponentially.

The results have been something less than disappointing — and the Church has continued in decline — because what we were really studying and working for was "church growth," not evangelism.

Church growth became our priority because membership was shrinking. We designed programs to reverse the trend. We filled conferences on the subject of church growth. We wanted the Church to grow, but we didn't want to do the work of an evangelist.

In spite of all the complex definitions we may have formulated, evangelism boils down to sharing what you know about Someone you love with someone else, so they can discover that love relationship, too. You cannot really love someone and keep it a secret. Infatuation is an intensely private matter, but true love is very public. A funny thing happens when you share your love for Christ Jesus (or for anyone in your life). As you speak of Him and all that He has done for you, you come to appreciate Him even more, and your love grows deeper.

For the sake of yourself and your own relationship with Jesus — as well as for the sake of your friends and neighbors who are lost and searching for the truth —

you must share your faith.

Christ has commanded you to take His Gospel into all the world. Evangelism is your part in the renewal of the Episcopal Church. A secret: healthy churches don't grow because they have used "right" techniques. People who love their *church* don't attract others to it. But people who love their *Lord* multiply churches — not by techniques, but by sharing *Whom* they know. This is your personal calling, too.

As thousands of committed Episcopal believers like you catch this vision for personal ministry and for the rebirth of the Episcopal Church, I believe our united work and prayer will bring about a new day for the Church. We must remember that there is no "righteous" Church — only God is righteous (Matthew 19:17). I have hope for the Church, not because of our righteousness, but because I deeply believe in the righteous Lord and Savior and His love for us.

My calling — and the calling of Episcopalians United — to foster reform, revival and renewal in the Episcopal Church remains strong. We are actively working toward these goals, relying on the Savior and the cooperation of believers like you. Billy Sunday once said, "The Episcopal Church is a slumbering giant. If it ever wakes up, we will see the seeds of revival sown in this country such as we have never, never seen before." That was powerful talk from one of our country's most popular evangelists. That future lies before us. The slumbering giant, of tortured rest, still lives in this broken but still redeemable body, the Episcopal Church. The day is surely on the horizon when the Episcopal Church claims its full heritage in Christ Jesus. That is the hope I live and work for, that I preach and teach.

I dream of that day.

I dream of the day when our bishops will be known as men and women of God who know and teach the Word of God. Who do you suppose is the most recognized Episcopal bishop today? Whose name have more people — Episcopalians and non-Episcopalians — heard on the television or seen on the newsstand?

Bishop John Spong — a man who repudiates the authority of God's Word and calls the Virgin Mary's Spirit-conceived Child a conception of rape. It's a sad day for the Episcopal Church that this is the bishop who has come to the fore. But I dream of a day, and I can envision its soon coming, when the bishops and priests of the Episcopal Church are again known as teachers of the Gospel, people who live and breathe the Scriptures, preaching and teaching them with excitement and authority.

I dream of that day.

I dream of the day that Episcopal laity will be known as the evangelists of our Church. I dream of the day when someone looks down the street, sees a couple of missionaries knocking on doors, and says, "Here come those Episcopalians again."

Right now the image of the Episcopal Church is either that of a prestigious denomination for the wealthy and powerful (a good many U.S. presidents have been Episcopalian) or that of a progressive, New Age church that welcomes and blesses homosexuality and allows the worship of others gods and goddesses. It's a sad day for the Episcopal Church when this is the opinion of many people — but I dream of a day when the word "Episcopalian" is synonymous with missionary and minister.

I believe God is preparing us for that time — everything is in place for that day. As you and thousands of like-minded believers accept the God-appointed calling of missionary and evangelist to your own family and community, that day will come.

I am dreaming of it already.

I think that's a bold vision, a vision for a renewed, indeed a *new* Church that will not only survive the 20th century, but will thrive in the 21st century. It is an exciting vision, one I believe Christ is calling the Episcopal Church toward. I can't see the entire vision for the Church yet. I need your vision, too. I won't always have the faith you have, and I'll need you to encourage me sometimes. You won't always have the drive I have, and you'll need me to strengthen you. We must learn to pray for one another — and to pray together. We must become better intercessors.

And we must persevere. The way forward is through perseverance, prayer, fellowship, bold witness — exciting stuff! But we need not persevere alone, as single individuals, bearing our own burdens. We must come together to encourage, support and educate one another, to share fellowship and study together.

I don't believe you and I can save the Episcopal Church — but I believe that Jesus Christ is able and willing to do so.

I don't believe our bishops will all suddenly get right with God and turn this Church around — but I believe that Jesus Christ wants the Church turned around. He's working *with* some of our bishops and working *on* others.

I don't think the priests will catch fire for the Gospel overnight and begin proclaiming its truth from the housetops — but I think Jesus wants this to happen. Our prayers and our witness will help. Hearts change slowly. But, they *do* change!

I don't believe our laity will awaken with a start out of their apathetic slumber because I want them to — but I believe they may awaken as we share a loving and vital faith with them.

Jesus is not going to let this once-dynamic Church settle into apathy, nor is He going to let us wax and wane into apostasy easily. No, Christ has called too many Episcopalians into His service — and equipped them to raise their voices and awaken the slumbering giant.

I have encouraged you to "throw off then everything that hinders and the sin that so easily entangles us" and "run with perseverance the race marked out for us." How do you run a race? Not by looking down at the ground and counting every step, but by keeping yourself focused on the goal. We'll change nothing in the Episcopal Church if we keep our eyes fixed on her present failings.

We will change everything in our lives, relationships and churches if we keep our eyes fixed on Jesus, the author and finisher of our faith. Again I say, we will run — and win — the race if we fix our eyes firmly on Him.

For the sake of the Episcopal Church we love, for the sake of the nation we love, for the sake of the world Christ loves and has called us to change, let us keep our eyes fixed on Him. Working and praying faithfully together, we will see Him transform us and our Church to His glory.

With renewed faith and confidence in our Lord and Savior, light a candle and pass along the flame. Together, and in time, we will cause new light to shine in the darkness that now besets our Church.